FINDING "ME"

INOCENCIA
TUPAS
MALUNES

◆ FriesenPress

Suite 300 - 990 Fort St
Victoria, BC, V8V 3K2
Canada

www.friesenpress.com

Copyright © 2020 by Inocencia Malunes
First Edition — 2020

Additional Contributors:
SANDRA LEE, who help me in the typing.
FERMIN RODRIGUEZ, my husband who along side with me all the way in giving me courage.

As a man thinketh, in his heart so is he what ever he thinks he will become. By: James Allen.

All rights reserved.

No part of this publication may be reproduced in any form, or by any means, electronic or mechanical, including photocopying, recording, or any information browsing, storage, or retrieval system, without permission in writing from FriesenPress.

ISBN
978-1-5255-6889-3 (Hardcover)
978-1-5255-6890-9 (Paperback)
978-1-5255-6891-6 (eBook)

1. BIOGRAPHY & AUTOBIOGRAPHY, PERSONAL MEMOIRS

Distributed to the trade by The Ingram Book Company

JANUARY 5, 2020

I am Inocencia Malunes. I was born in the Philippines. I am the fourth of six siblings, having four sisters and a brother. We live in a farming community with my parents. our livelihood depends mostly on harvesting crops on other people's farms because, although my parent's family has a small rice farm, there are seven in the family, and there is a rotation in cultivating the farm.

My father, being the fourth one in the family, has to wait four years before he has his turn. The good thing is that he is in charge of a small fishpond that he has to cultivate every three months. But, for our rice, my three older sisters have to travel far and wide—to wherever other people's farms that are ready to be harvested—so they can help in the work. Whatever their shares are accumulate for our month's use until another farm is ready to harvest. My mother has a talent in making dresses, so most of the people in the community have something for her to sew, and she has a green thumb for cultivating her small vegetables garden that she depends on for our food and for money to spend.

Having eight of us in the family life is very tough, and at a young age I have already my schedule to take care of the pig; that alone can help my parents with the cost of our school supplies and other expenses. As we are growing up, my parents feel the hardship of having so many kids to raise, and one day, my mother tells me that my father and she have decided to give me away to a couple our distance relatives who have no kids of their own.

At this time, I am four or five years old. Of course, I am so surprised to hear this news, and at that age, you remember everything, so I question her about why. She says to me that this couple has money, and they can afford to send me to school and even to University and because I am vivacious. She says that one day I could have a job, so I could help my sisters and brother with their school or life. But I protest and ask her if I am not her child. So, she has more explanation, but I don't want to listen. I ask her not to give me away because I will try my very best. I will study hard and harder so that I can find a job to help them.

Our life gets tougher every day as the community grows. But that conversation between my mother and me has gone quickly in the thin air, at least for me. Until one day comes and this couple come to our house, and our story comes to its fruition. I am so sad and crying at the same time, but it's time to go. From our house, it's about half a kilometer from the open ocean where they left their speed boat. What this couple doesn't know is that I have a plan of my own. Even though I am still crying, when they are about to start the engine, I jump off the boat. I almost drown, so the couple has no choice but to bring me back home. So, that is the end of my mother's story and me.

Our lives go back to normal, but the trauma that I experienced shattered me inside No one can put it back together again but me. I did not cause harm to my mother for I understood her motive, which was for my own good and for the good of everyone. My promise to my mother is printed deep in my heart, and no matter what, I will strive forward to keep that promise to her.

Time passes by, and life gets tougher and tougher everyday, but our routine has to continue. While we are growing up, the expectation of the siblings is harder every day.

I am always with my mother whenever she goes to the market to sell her produce, whether fish or vegetable. I am always with her so I can be handy to help, whatever the task may be.

One day, it happened again. One of our distant relatives, a couple with two young children, whose names are Stella and Stephen arrive. It is the school year closing, so for two months, I have to spend my time looking after these kids.

At this time, I am seven years old. When the children are asleep, I am faced with two basins of dirty clothes to wash. I don't really know how I was able to keep up with all of the chores, but days just glided away one to the next; I didn't notice that two months had quickly passed until my older sister Gloria picked me up from the city, and I was home again and ready for school.

I don't really know if I made money from that experience of two months away from home. Back to normal again. I am always studying; my grades never go down from eighty-five. But when I am in the ninth grade, I get ninety-five but never get an honor at grade school.

The routine in my family is the same; I am always with my mother. Whatever she does, I am always ready to help her. One time, we go to the beach to gather some baby oysters and all the kinds of shellfish that we can find. Most of the time when I see an airplane passing by, I stand up, looking and looking until it vanishes into thin air and telling myself that one day an airplane will take me somewhere. I don't know where, but I can feel it and really believe it. My mother always reminds me that the high tide will soon be coming, and we don't have much in our basket. I am kind of a dreamy child; I have lots of things I have to do when I grow up. When I was still small, I could not resist going to the farm where I heard the frogs croaking. I was so fascinated by tadpoles that I would play with them for hours. When I came home, my sister Gloria would pinch me and grab me to have a bath quickly because no one could stand the smell of the frog on me But now, I know the messages of this animal and why I was so attracted to them; they represented "abundance" to me.

Now that my parents have no means, I cannot go to high school to continue any studies. I have to go back to my schedule of taking care of the pigs. By this time, I have two of them. Time goes mostly to the preparation of feeding these two pigs, once in the morning and once at noontime. I have to give them a bath before feeding them so on the evening and that's nonstop it seems lost. I am so attached to these two animals that they become my pets. My mother tells me that when the pigs are the age of six months, she is going to sell one so she can have some money to use.

When the time comes that the buyer comes to the house, I have to go somewhere far away so I couldn't hear the cry of the pig. I can't let it go, they are each a part of me. This life of mine goes on for at least two years, then, one day, my mother gathers us—all three of my sisters and me—to inform us that she has some amount of money to send one of us to high school. She has decided that I will be the one to go first because she needs my three older sisters to gather more rice during the harvest season for our food, and the other one has to look after another pig that mother is getting.

My school goes smoothly for the first six month. My tuition fees are on time, and my allowance for the bus fare, from her vegetable garden harvest, is plentiful.

I really try to study hard , so I can get an honor, which will provide free tuition for the next year; and so it happens, but I get only third, which does not even qualify. For the second year, I can't go to school because my mother has run out of money, but I tell her not to worry about it. I am planning to find a job in the city, whatever job it may be, just as long as I'm not wasting any time that year. But, instead, my sister Gloria is able to find a job in the city, where they sell all kinds of goods from clothing to household materials. On her way home, she saw a Wanted sign in the window of one of the restaurants in that area. So she was able to ask the owner if she could recommend one of her sisters for work there. The owner says yes, if she could bring her sister tomorrow.

So, she told my mother. As always, I am the one that is picked. I don't have any idea what my sister arranged with the owner—if I have a salary how much the salary might be, I don't know. All I do is just work. I am fifteen years old by this time. I do all kind of work at the restaurant, and it's so busy everyday. We can't sit down for a minute because their place is in the center of the entrance to the market, which makes it the first restaurant that the people can see. I learn to like my job. Talking to different people, young and old, is a pleasure for me. I am well acquainted with Melly, the daughter of the owner , and she is in charge of the money. She puts it only on the big box in the corner and, most of the time, I have to tell her that the money is already overflowed and some is on the floor. It's really so busy that her mother and father help us a lot by measuring the foods that we serve.

During the nighttime, after closing, I have to go home with her mother and father, with the cook and the dishwasher. But Melly, the daughter, lives in her auntie's house. They are a well-off family. They are business-oriented people. The aunt and the uncle own a big tailoring business too.

I have worked in the restaurant for quite sometimes now, and I love the life in the city, although I don't have time to explore the city during the daytime, and I don't have a day off. It doesn't bother me at all because, some of the nights, Melly and I go to the movie house.

This family has ten siblings and only one brother like my family. Most of the young ones are in school and university, so we can see each other at night. They treat me like their own. Until one day, I had an accident. I was filling the gallon-size glass of water when, all of the sudden, it just broke in half; the top landed right on top of my right foot. The security quickly picked me up and got me to the ambulance right away. Melly went with me to the hospital where I got five stitches to close up my cut.

From the hospital, they bring me to her aunt's big house, and my mother and sister come for a visit. Since I can't go to work, they tell my mother that I'll stay there until my foot heals.

Three months pass so quickly. Because of the deep wound on my right foot, it's still difficult for me to walk, and my mother and father have decided to bring me home. I was not able to go back to work. I found out from my mother that for my work for the entire year, the owner of the restaurant is been paying me fifteen Philippine pesos a month. My sister Gloria has been the one collecting my salary and giving it all to my mother. As for me, I don't really mind about the money. My mother has sewn a new dress for me, and I am so happy for that. My mother is a very religious mother. Every Sunday when we were growing up, we attended mass except for my father, because of his livelihood that early in the morning either or the fish pond he is ready himself to climb up the coconut tree to gather the coconut sap that my uncle has to pay him for doing that in his entire life, for making that a vinegar or selling that in the city for drinking. At this time, my sister Gloria still works in the city, and I ask her if my employer is still waiting for me. She tells me that all the restaurant around that area have to close. For sanitation reasons, the government is changing the setting so all the restaurants will be in the center of the central market.

At this time, since I am no longer working, I am helping my mother tend her vegetable garden. My sister Vivina has one water buffalo and two cows to look after. We have to help one another to do all kinds of work, so we can survive like everyone else in our neighborhood. It's the beginning of the school year, and my mother allows me to enroll for my second year in high school. The name of the school that I'm attending is Negros Institute of Technology. It is located in Bacolod City, which is about half-an-hour travel by jeepney or thirteen kilometers away from our home.

Everything goes smoothly in my studies in the beginning of six months. My tuition fees are not too expensive, but my allowance for my everyday commute is a problem because sometimes, my mother runs out of money, especially if she was not able to go to the market to sell her vegetables. In that case, on my way home, I wait for the jeepney that belongs to our distance relatives, and I ask him if he will allow me to ride—that I will pay him the next morning. This idea has nothing to do with my mother, but I have no choice.

There are times that this relative drops by my aunt's house, and he asks her the name of her niece who, most of the time, asks if he'll allow her to ride home and pay tomorrow. He says, "she really does pay me." But my aunt couldn't figure who it might be, so one day when she came to our house, she asked.

It happened that I was there, and I quickly said, "I am, and what else could I do? I have no money, and I keep my promise to pay him the next morning. That's how everyone knows it." She says I was so daring, but I answer her that you do what you have to do, and that's it.

I use only one pair of shoes that year for, if possible, I don't give my parents any trouble. I know already how much they struggle with raising us all. So, instead, I buy a needle and some thread so I can fix my shoes myself. That saves me money and my shoes last for one year. At that time, my younger sister, Flordeliza, is in first year high school too. There's a new school that is run by the catholic nuns in the town next to ours and my mother is able to enroll her. So, she is able to finish her high school there. The name of the school she goes to is Holy Family High School.

As for me, at the end of that school year, I have to find work in the city. One day, when I come home from work, my mother tells me that Melly had come looking for me. She is the daughter of my employer who owns the restaurant in the central market, and I know, for sure, that she had a hard time finding our town because it's the first time that she has come to our house. Of course, she found out how poor our living condition is. My mother says to me that she sensed a surprised look on Melly's face, but she gave my mother her address where I can find her. This is the beginning of another experience and learning of the next journey of my life.

Melly is already married at this time, and she owns a kitchenette at the other side entrance of my high school. I am so happy because I don't have to travel far away. I pack up my things, and here I go again! There are six of us working in the restaurant, and two of us are going to school. One is a boy whose sister is working with us too. He is here as dishwasher, and he is a first-year high schooler. Everyone is so busy on their assignments early in the morning. Melly and I and the two girls go to the market to buy all kinds of vegetables and all kinds of different foods and ingredients for our menu of the day. Plus, we have our everyday chores, but we all get along so smoothly.

As far as my studies go, I have to enroll at night school, so I suppose that means two years more. It goes to three years to finish because I couldn't take all my subjects, but that's alright with me because I always bargain my education for my service. I don't have a salary or an allowance, but Melly is open to give me whatever I need for expenses at school. That's fine because I don't need to give money to my parents at this time. I have to survive on my own while I am studying, but deep inside of me, I don't forget my promise to my mother.

We have been doing business in that place for two years. Melly got pregnant and, because she is already in her late age of productivity, the doctor advised her to stop working in order to get this child. She has to travel to Manila to stay with her older sister because the doctor specialist is in Manila.

Her husband Edgar has to travel there, but he will just drop her off because he is working in the sugar milling company here in the city. So, I am in charge of running the kitchenette for the time being. I am already trained on the menu of the business, all kinds of food that we prepare for that day, and we don't lose any customers because they are all students in the school, and we have the student boarder. The six of us get along very well, and Melly's husband doesn't bother us. He just asks me every day if I have enough money to spend on the expenses, and I say yes. When I show him my collection for the day, I can see the surprise in his eyes, and I know he trusts me too.

Six months have passed by, and it's time for Melly to come home. Edgar has to go to Manila to pick her up. I give him some cash, but I put it in the record so I can give it to Melly when she comes home. It's really an experience running a restaurant without the eyes of your employer. It is really a test of time, character, and trust— all at the same time. One thing I can say, I did it all and it's a big credit for myself. I am so proud of myself. I know now that I am capable of doing something without knowing exactly how to do it. It's so amazing, and I love myself for that.

When Melly arrives home, we are so happy to see her. Her pregnancy has gotten bigger over the past six months, so we don't allow her to move around. She just sits in the corner to accept the money. And when I give her all the money that we earned for the six months that she was away, she is so proud of us for our capacity to run her business without her. We took care of it very well, and she is so happy and proud of us all. Mostly on the weekends, I go home to visit my family on the farm. Most of the time when I go, the house is empty like no one is at home. Everyone has to find a way to look for means that they can contribute to help the family to survive. One weekend, I find my mother in her vegetable garden, and instead of helping her, I am carried away by my amazement of so many dragonflies. I couldn't help myself chasing and catching them, especially the red and the green ones. I know these insects have a message for us.

We are able to run the restaurant for a year more when Melly goes back to Manila to have her baby. One of the girls that works with us has to leave, so only five of us run the business. It's a bit hectic for all of us because the reassignment of chores are added to my work, but still we manage it all. It's not an easy task running a business at such a young age, especially without the owner. It requires quite a lot of knowledge to handle, but I am surprised how well we managed it all.

There are times when I stop and think and wonder about some higher power that is inside of our bodies and that does all these tasks that we do. Otherwise, how can we do them without exhaustion? I say to myself, "Someday, I will be the one to find out the truth to all this."

The time has come! Melly has come home with her beautiful girl. She is so precious that the girls are glued to her. It's amazing how fast the days glide away; six months have passed. The place is not big enough to accommodate us all, and Melly and her husband, Edgar, have decided to close the restaurant,. She let everybody go except me. It is the closing of the school year.

We have to move where her husband works in the sugar milling compound, which is in another city and about forty-five minutes to the school. Where I study, luckily, there is a school bus that picks up all the students at night. My work is lighter than it used to be because I just look after the baby. Her name is Emily; she is such an adorable girl, and I am never tired of her. After I feed her and put her to sleep, I do the house chores—washing the clothes, cooking, cleaning the house. We live in one bedroom of a big house. The upper part is occupied by the clinic's family nurse who works for the whole compound. On the opposite side of where we are, there is a two-bedroom in which a family of three people—the mother and two daughters lives. I don't have a room of my own, so at night, I have to gather all six chairs that belong to our dining table and put a mat on top of them. This is where I sleep.

I manage everything as if it's normal for the sake of my studies, so I can finish my high school at that time. I am already in my fourth year. Melly has to go to Bacolod City to help her parents run the coffee shop. It is now in a different area, one that is very close to where all the hardware stores are. Everyday customers are so the same everyday customers are the same as all the employees, which is not bad because it is steady.

Time passes by, and I am in my last year of my school. I don't worry for my bus because Edgar has to get me a bus pass for the whole year. They don't give me any money if I don't have any project to school, and I don't ask them for an allowance. Sometimes, if Melly gives me some amount, I keep it for emergency expenses, but there are times that I give it back to her if she needs it. We all get along in the house, helping one another, and they both treat me like their family.

On the weekend, sometimes they allow me to visit home, and I ask my mother to make me a new dress. If she has extra money, she goes to the market right away and buys the materials.

She can sew it right away. None of my older sisters have gone to high school; they just finished their grade school because my parents have no means, and everyone knows that.

Back home with my employer, I am so happy to think that I am finishing my school year, but at the same time, I wonder what will be the next stage of my life journey. I know they could not afford to send me to university because Emily is growing up, and they don't have an extra income to spend on me. I understand that because I can see the situation; at the same time, they have told me this.

My school year's end comes, and I have to stay with them for a while because of Emily. I can't leave her because Melly still needs me look after Emily. She is two and a half years old by now. And I want to be with them until Melly tells me that they don't need me anymore. I know she won't do that; instead, she will wait for me to say it myself.

It happens that one of her sisters in New York has her vacation, and she is able to visit us. I heard her talking, saying that she is planning to sponsor them so they can go to Canada because their only brother lives in Toronto. If they go, they will help him with the expenses.

I know the immigration will push through because, at that time, it's easier to process the papers than now because they need immigrants to come. We talk about immigration, but they can't take me with them, so I ask Melly if she will allow me to start looking for other work, and she does. I don't have any idea what I am going to do, but while I am wandering around in the city, I come across one of my classmates, Ofelia. We have a little chat, and I ask her where she works. She tells me in the Visayan

Packing Corporation canning factory down in Mandalagan. I ask her if she could help me find a job there.

I am able to find her company and she had told me where to apply. I have no doubt that I will land a job there one day because she told me that around 510 people work there in different departments. She lent me her white uniform, and she gave me the directions for where to apply. I will go there everyday; the person who is accepts applications is Robert Sevilleno.

One day when I am in the hiring office with no other applicants, he asks me how I know that the company is hiring. I say, "I don't know, but maybe you need some people." He just turns his head from me. I will stay there for a while because Ofelia has already told me his style. I plan to be there everyday without knowing that I will be hired. And that goes on for one month. No one talks to me in his office, but I never give up. I know I need a job, and I need it now.

One day he comes in, and I know he is not in good mood because it shows in his face. I am just standing there and he says all of a sudden: "You again?"

And I say, "Yes, sir, because I really need to work." He just passes me by. I can't remember how many times this has already happened, but I don't mind at all. I am about to leave, but something inside of me tells me to wait.

When he comes out of his office, he says to me, "If you really want to work, go and change your uniform. So, I go to the washroom and come out wearing my uniform. I go back into his office and he calls his assistant to guide me into the factory line.

On my first day at work, I can't explain my feelings about facing so many women workers. I sit down with the ladies. That morning, they are picking some bad or defective white beans that're for making the pork and beans in the can. In our break time, I see my classmate who helped me with everything, and we pretend that we don't know each other. That goes on for quite sometime. I am still living with Melly, and she is happy that I got a job. She is already getting her family's paperwork in order to travel to Canada, and she is the one looking after her daughter when I am at work. Months have gone by, and I am steady in my work in the city, and Melly and her family have already completed their papers to travel abroad. I tell her, "Who knows, one day we will see each other in Canada under one roof again," and we laugh.

Before they set off on their travels, I ask permission to leave home, so I can find a place to live close to where I work. She and her husband agree with me. I live where my friend Ofelia lives. Including me, we are fourteen ladies living in the same boarding house. I know I have to get along with these people in order for me to stay here. Since Ofelia has been with these ladies for years, they work in groups, some have four and others have three. They ask me if I want to be in one group, but I tell them, I can manage by myself at least for now. I will try to make it on my own, and so I did.

I have to get up so early, about 3:00 a.m., to prepare my food for the morning and for noon time so that when I come home for lunchtime, I have something to eat that I don't need to cook. I manage comfortably at work and at the boarding house. There are times when I buy some tuna heads, which cost me twenty-five cents a kilo and with one head weighing about three kilos to four kilos. I have to go home to my parent's house to bring these tuna heads to them, and my father and mother are so happy that I can see the happiness on their faces. I know they are very proud of me.

Most of the time when I visit home, my mother lets me take lots of vegetables from the garden and some rice so I don't need to buy any for the boarding house. I am so happy to think that, at this time, I am able to start keeping my promise to help that I made to my mother . And so, I'll just do the best I can to not make any mistakes at work, so I can keep my work for a longer time.

In the factory, there are lots of departments. They have tin cans, labeling sardines and squid canning, pork and beans, and Frankfort or sausage departments. They also have a department where they pack prawns. When I was there for two years, the founder transferred me to the sausage department as a weigher.

I have to weigh fourteen ingredients. Two of us are assigned as weighers, and my shift, most of the time, is in the morning for eight hours. I like that because my uniform is very clean, and I don't have to change it everyday. In that department, we also produce cured ham. Lots of people buy the whole legs to bring home, and some people buy the sliced one by the kilo. Sometimes, I have to buy some pork ribs and tuna heads, if not the sausage trimmings, and bring them home to my parents. At the same time, I can go back to my boarding house quickly for its only half an hour travel by the jeepney. During my days off, I feel like doing overtime, and I leave my name with security at the entrance gate for whichever department needs people early in the morning. Almost all my off days, I work. Our salary rate is based on an hourly rate at the cannery. When I started, they paid us seventy-nine cents an hour, but at the sausage department, our rate is $1.10 that is one peso and ten cents. So, it's much higher than the cannery. On my payday, usually I just keep the amount for my expenses at the boarding house, for the room and food. The rest I don't even count. I just go home and give it to my mother, and sometimes she has a surprise for me. I have three new dresses that she made for me, and I'm very happy for that.

Time passes by, and because I am consumed by working so much, it pops into my mind to visit Melly, just to say hello to the two kids. I'm so glad that I am able to see them before they fly to Canada. I have to return home quickly because the travel time is forty-five minutes, and if I miss the bus, it takes some time to wait for another one.

When I trace all the dots in my journey of life and see that they are all connected to one another, it's like a dream for me. I am able to show my mother that I am serious about keeping my promise to her to help my parents and my siblings. My work is steady. It's the source of everything I have, but I have no savings because I give all the money to my mother. It hasn't occurred to me to save because I thought that this factory would be here forever and because I have been settled here for years and years. There is some gossip that I hear from my coworkers that the owner of this factory has passed it on to his son to manage, so there must be some changes. I don't focus any attention on these stories.

My work is still stable. It is now my fifth year in this work, and I don't worry about anything. I just continue my work. At this time, my mother is not feeling well, and she lost a lot of weight. My two sisters Gloria and Rosalinda take her to the doctor and, according to them, she has not been well. They have to wait for the results, but the support that I have given her helps a lot for their expenses. So, I just keep going to my work. Worries and fears are not a part of me, and I focus my thinking purely on my work—that I will not lose it. For my job is my only source of income for myself and for my help to my family. The day comes with the result of my mother's diagnosis, and it is ovarian cancer. They need her to have an operation right away, but the support that I am giving them is not enough, and my father has to sell one of their water buffalo to survive their expenses. My work is still in good standing, and I can still support my life in the city, although most of my income goes back home to keep them. What will happen to my mother? I don't feel any worry or fear at all. I think that she will survive it for she is a very religious woman, and I know she has the favor of the higher power or intelligence. At the end of each work shift, I have to go home to visit her and everybody. It seems that she gets much better every day, and I keep her in my prayers all the time. Even when I am at work, my mind is always with her in prayer. Months pass, and she is already walking outside to get some morning sunshine. She has gained a little bit of weight, and I am so happy to see her after work. At home, no one calls me by my name; they call me one Neneng, which is the nickname that my mother and father gave me. So, everyone calls me that name.

One time, on my day off, instead of doing overtime, I go home. I stop by the market to buy lots of goodies for my mother, and she thanks me, saying that she is so proud of me, that I am a very responsible person, and that I have helped them a lot. She mentions to me that she misses tending her vegetable garden, and I tell her that her garden will be there when she is healed.

The new management has already taken effect at work, and there has been no change for the product that we work with everyday. By now, we are already receiving two pesos an hour salary. In the department I work in, we are all in rotation because we have a demo for our product. This means that, some days, six of us are assigned to the field—we have to sell our product until they close our department, which means that we have to come back to the cannery department. This is no problem for me because I need more money than ever for my mother depends on me for all her expenses for doctor visits and follow-ups. It is my day off, so the day before, I go home after work and bring all my dirty uniforms with me to wash. After lunch, I fall asleep, and I have a vivid dream. In my dream, there is a very heavy rain, and I run quickly. I pass my mother who is sleeping on the floor, and she is disturbed. She asks me what happened. I tell her that I have a dream in which there's a heavy rain, so I run to gather my laundry. But, it is a bright, sunny day.

And she says to me, "Oh! Neneng. I will be gone soon."

I say back to her, "Don't say that," but she says that's the meaning of your dream. I know my mother. She is a very intuitive person, and I just pray that it won't happen. I still have one day more to stay at home and to be with my mother, to help her be outside to get some sunshine in the morning. It is important for me to be home at this time, so I can see all my siblings together at the table at lunch and dinnertime.

At work, there are some changes happening. It's December, and lots of trucks are arriving with a lot of goods that are being unloaded. I cannot see what's going on. There are boxes upon boxes, and they go right in the storage. During the first week of December, they pick some girls, but only the girls who can work by the storage, and no one is opening their mouths about what's going on. I don't have any idea. On that day, I am working with one of my chemists whose name is Myrna Ercilla. She is experimenting, trying to make some candy out of flour and chickpeas. I have been working with her for three days, doing all the weighing of all the ingredients that she needed when there is a call from the office. They tell me to go home quickly because my mother has passed away. I am in total shock. I don't know what happened to all the ingredients that I have been weighing. I run like a jet. But when I get home, my mother is gone. It is the saddest moment that I have experienced in my life. Everything that I have hoped for is all just gone, all of what I have gone through, my hard work, and all my sacrifices are all washed away. Life for me and living have no meaning at all.

But what about my promise that I made to my mother long ago? Was that not a commitment to honor my word now that she is gone? I thought so, and so life must go on. My mother is only forty-nine years old when she passes away. I go back to work to sign out for a week's vacation until my mother is buried. We don't have any money for the funeral; I don't have any savings because I gave all my salary to my father for their expenses for the hospital, food, and medicine for my mother. So, my father gets a loan from one of the farmers in our town. The farmer gets the water buffalo to work on his farm until my father returns the amount of money and can get back the water buffalo.

My sister Flordeliza is already working with Doctora Esteban in Bacolod City. She has to help set up her clinic in the morning and, after that, she works in the house in exchange for her studies. She is taking midwifery at River Side Hospital where her employer has a clinic as a dermatologist. My sister is able to borrow money from her employer and with that amount, my father is able to free the water buffalo from working long hours on the field in order for us to survive for the funeral of our beloved mother.

My life at work is much tougher than it used to be. Everyone must survive every day. Our schedule keeps changing from department to department. It doesn't surprise me at all because if it's new management, there's always a change. Our product is now mostly toys—different and all kinds of toys—and who knows where they come from. It's close to Christmastime, so I am able to purchase some toys for my younger and only brother who my mother loved most. He was only ten years old when my mother passed away.

Our father does his best to keep us together when we are all at home. He still looks after the fish pond with the help of my baby brother and tends the farm with the help of my two sister when it's his turn. He gives up climbing the coconut tree to collect the coconut sap because, now that our mother's gone, nobody will record how many litters he collects everyday .

At this time, our sister Gloria gets married. She and her husband live separately from us, but they have their little shack not far from us. Her husband does carpentry work, and my sister still works where she used to work in the city.

Now that we are mature, each one must find her own way, but still I keep my responsibility to give some amount of money to my father for their expenses. Now I am able to save a small amount for myself. I learn my lesson this time, and I feel that we are all on shaky ground at work now. All are still in the schedule, but the changes are unbelievable. The atmosphere is much more difficult than it used to be. I note that something will happen, but you don't know when. The first department that closes is the tin can department since the stock that they are just finishing is for some pork and beans canning. The prawns packing is still operating.

I have no more overtime, and my day off is more now to spent that the busiest time I use to be is over—gone completely. We still enjoy our life in the factory and every week on our day off, when the most girls are off, we plan a field trip, and that's why we can visit lots of different places in our province that we have never been to before.

I am always on the lookout for whatever will happen at work, so I will be prepared for my next move. I can't afford to be jobless now that my mother is gone; they now need me more than ever for my financial help at home. I notice that not far from our boarding house is a cottage industry. I notice that a few ladies carry some materials for making a curtain and bedcover and seat cover. So, one afternoon after my shift and on my way home, I drop by just to say hello to the two ladies who are sewing something by the window, see how they do it, and make a friend. I introduce myself, and I tell them that I live just three houses away from them. They know my landlady because she has ordered some pillowcases and bedcover from them. They know her, so every time I finish my work, I wave to them on my way home.

The office hasn't given us notice yet what will happen to the factory, but we hear some rumors that it will be sold to the Japanese investor who will convert it to a television assembly plant. We are not sure when it might happen because we haven't had a meeting yet. So I am still scheduled for packing toys, which I love because I have never seen this many different kinds of toys in my life. When we were growing up, we could hardly buy our food, let alone toys. And I feel so privileged to have them in my hands, even though I'm just packing them. There are times that, when we finish packaging, we have to go to the labeling department.

One day, when I am walking home to the boarding house, I meet Ninfa, the lady who works in the cottage industry. She tells me that she is planning to separate from that work because, she says, she knows how to make all these things, and she is ready to find her own customers, so she can be independent. I tell her that's a very clever idea, and she asks me if I know some place that she could rent. I say no because I am not familiar with the neighborhood. She says that maybe one day I could help her if she is already on her own, and I say I would love to.

I am twenty-one years old now and have worked here in the factory for more than five years now. I am so thankful for my work, that it has supported me and my family. At this time, I have to be prepared for what might happen at my work. I have some little amount for my savings, which I can spend if I need to look for another job. I visit home once in a while, but I seldom see my sister Flordeliza who is in the last year of her school course although she lives here in the city. She is very busy with her work and study. My younger brother Norberto is in the high school where we live. At this time, he only gradual they build first year and every year the build another one for the second year and so on.

Our father is focusing only on the fish pond. He gave up his turn toiling the farm. Instead, one of his brothers will work my father's turn, then he will just give my father a share of three sacks of rice. That is enough for both of them and for my sister Rosalinda. She is working out of town and is not married at this time.

At work, they call for the meeting where they tell us that our operation will last only for two months. We have to prepare because the factory will be closed. Some of the ladies who live at the boarding house don't even wait for the two months. They start leaving one by one, some of them live as far away as another province. So, I contact the lady in the cottage industry to see if she is still looking for a place because maybe, if she would like to live here where we are, she can talk to our landlady. Out of fourteen of us in the boarding house, only six leave. I want to stay at my job to the end— besides, I do not live far away from home. And now, I have a prospect for another job in the case that Ninfa decides to separate from her employer. I can be of help to her until I can get some training for that kind of work.

So, the time has come, and after all the long years of working here, I am jobless again. I don't worry. I have a little bit of savings that I can use while I look for another job in the city, but I decide to take it easy. I go to visit Melly's family; they have not yet gone abroad, but she tells me that it won't be long now. They are just waiting for her brother from Toronto to pick them up to travel. So, we have a little chat, and I tell her that the factory has closed because it has been sold to a Japanese business for an electronic assembly plant.

Melly assures me that she is not worried about me finding a job soon because she knows that I am so restless to find work if I need it. And, when I am ready, I will work non-stop to find one. I tell her that if I am not able to see them when it's their time to travel abroad, I wish them all the best for their journey and new beginning in another country, and one day, I will see them again.

That is the reason, my dear readers, whoever you are, whatever circumstances you may be in, you don't have to worry. We are not in charge our own destinies; there is a Higher Intelligence inside of us—all that original love, power, and light that lightens us all when we come to this earth. All we must do is, first, love our selves; second, follow our heart's desires; and third, trust yourselves. Most of all, you must believe in you! Because knowing who you really are is your saviour from poverty and hardship, and it will lead you to prosperity and abundance for I am, you, and me are one.

I am staying at home for awhile, just to try to clear my mind and to decide what my next move will be. It is a rainy season, so my thought is to spread the baby plant the banana plants, Those were the fruit that saved us from hunger when we were growing up. Banana plants supported my parents providing food and money that they could use. My father is really very pleased that I am staying home, so I can cook for my younger brother and him while he is working in the fish pond. My younger sister Flordeliza visits us once a month. She is working at her employer's and finishing her school. My older sister Rosalinda is also working in Manila. She never sends us money because she is saving it. When she comes home, she can buy some presents for everybody. She will come only once a year, but she gives much to my father.

I go to the city to buy some of our groceries and while I am walking, l hear someone call my name. When I turn back, it's the lady who is working in the cottage industry. She has already talked to my landlady, and she is going to rent the upper room where our landlady used to stay But the landlady is no longer living there, so she is going to rent out the whole house. She is moving to another property that she is able to buy.

So Ninfa asks me if I am willing to help her start her business. Since I am free, I tell her that I am willing to help. We don't talk about the salary she could afford to give me because she is just starting. When I get home, I tell my father the good news—that I have another prospect and I can gain another skill for making money some day. And so, here I am again, packing up my things to go back to where I was before—the same house but this time upstairs. I tell Ninfa about my plan that she won't have to pay me a salary while I am still learning. By the time that I learn, we will have already have built up our customer base, then she could allow me to go back to school to take a night class, and she agrees.

The house has been occupied by three different tenants in the basement where I used to live with thirteen other ladies. Now it is rented by a couple with two kids. She is working as a dressmaker, and her husband is working in the factory where I used to work; he is the maintenance man of the building. In the upstairs' room beside ours, is new couple working in the radio station DYKB. We get along, sharing the kitchen and the living room, and Ninfa has one sewing machine for making curtains, bedcovers, seat covers, and pillowcases.

Most of the customers we get are through word of mouth from the store where we buy our cloth. Most of the customers ask the store clerks who they know that can sew these things. I have to learn how to estimate how much material we need by computing the width of the cloth and considering the width of the window that is to be covered by the curtain. We have to give an allowance because some of the cloth shrinks.

But for the seat covers, I give that to Ninfa. At the beginning, we are so peaceful because we can concentrate on our work. Our customers increase, and it's really a good business for making money quickly because these people are very rich.

The opening of the school year has come, but I don't start my school yet. One of Ninfa's brothers and one sister arrived to stay with us so they could study. The girl's name is Elena, and she is in her first year of high school. The boy, Sunday, is in grade six of elementary school. Since we have only one bedroom, three of us sleep in the bedroom, and the boy sleeps in the living room. I know it is not pleasant for the couple who share the living room with us.

Our work is increasing because Ninfa's popularity is much expanded because of recommendations from the customers who have seen her work and that lots of rich people like. During this time, she hires someone, and she buys another sewing machine. She gets another lady, whose name is Rosenda, who also worked in the place where she worked before. The couple that lived next door to us has moved out. I don't know the reason, but I figure the inconvenience that they suffered with us and being so crowded in the house are probably why. So, Ninfa occupies the whole upper house, and Rosenda and Elena can stay in the other room.

The best part of this job, the part I like the most, is when we deliver all this stuff to the owner. I am just mesmerized by the beauty of their houses, which are huge like castles, and all the fancy things that they display. It is just a privilege and a dream come true to be inside of these houses. My inspiration grows and grows, but I keep it to myself. There are days and night that we work nonstop—until we finish the work for delivery and that the owner needed delivered because they are hosting some occasion.

By the opening of the school year, I am able to enroll at the Osaka Institute of Technology. I am taking the Radio Telegraph Operator course. It's a two-year course. Everybody is getting along, although the house is so crowded. But it is no problem. When Ninfa's brother and sister are at school, we have more time to chat one another. Ninfa always has a new customer that is introduced by another when we deliver our work to her house. I just wish that someday I can have a business like this one. It's easy money if you do your own work, and if the customer loves it, the work is nonstop.

Every day in the afternoon, I have to prepare myself for school. I am so happy that I'm studying again. Most of our classmates are boys; only three of us are ladies and, of course, we must pay attention all the time because there are thirty-two in the class. You have to be attentive all the time because, if not, you'll be left behind. All subjects in Morse code are good.

I have passed my first year, and I have visited them at home a few times, but they are happy for me—that somehow, I am able to study again. My sister Rosalinda has already come home from Manila, and she put up a small store very close to our aunt's house that's close to high school in Sum-ag, about ten minutes travel from our town. She is doing well with a little business, so she is the one giving all the help for the expenses at home.

My father, at this time, is not in good shape for he has bad arthritis and pain in his hands and feet. My younger brother, when he is off school, helps by doing most of the work in the fish pond.

FINDING "ME"

When we don't have a rush delivery for our work, all of us go home and have an excursion by the ocean. It's not far from our home, and we cook lots of food from our house and take it with us to the beach where we stay there for a whole day of swimming. I love that part of our life, being carefree and just enjoying the time. But there can be just a few times that will happen because of my obligation to finish school.

At work, helping Ninfa with her business, customers are plentiful and so is the income. Although I don't have money in my pocket, when it's time for my exams and I need to pay my tuition I just ask Ninfa for money, and she always gives it to me, no problem. I almost become a part of her family, although there are more siblings. Most of her brothers and sisters are at their parent's house, and two are in Manila, working in factories according to her. When her father and mother visit with us, they treat me like their own daughter; they are very nice people. There are times when I bring them to our house and introduce them to my father, and they have a good time telling their own stories to one another. At the same time, they enjoy the open-air atmosphere, out of the city where you can smell the fresh air.

As the year goes by, I don't even have to wait for my school to finish. Days just glide by, and all of us in that class have passed our class year. Everyone is preparing for the board exam to be held in the city for that year, and so I have to spend most of the nights doing my review to refresh my memory. It is very difficult because we don't know the type of exams that they will give us and because we don't have a handout of the questions that we need to study.

One week before the exam begins, lots of students arrive in the city from all over the country. Most of the school has to be occupied by the student to be their lodging place to stay for two days before the exam starts. I am so excited, but at the same time, I feel a fear inside me and think that I might not pass the exam. The two ladies, my classmates, and I are always in contact; asking what subject we will study more for our review.

During the examination day, we have a designated chair to sit that has our name on it. So, I don't see any of my classmate in the room I'm in. It's a terrifying experience for me; my heart's pumping so hard because this is my first experience of attending a board exam for the whole country. The questionnaire is not easy, and I expected that, but the time limit that is given to us to answer every question is the scariest thing I have experienced.

As a whole, the examination lasts for a day because the examiner has to transfer from room to room after one group is done. My nightmare is gone, but it is printed deep inside my heart. We must wait for three months before the results will be announced in the newspaper. I am not excited for the result anymore because I am not sure if I passed or not. For now, my life must go on.

I met a lady during the exam whose name is Janet Bautista. She is not from where we live, but I have her phone number. We are in contact with one another, and one day she drops by and asks me if I want to come with her to the compound where I used to work in the factory. I say yes, so we go.

She tells me that she has been working in that TV and radio assembly plant for about one year, but this time we are going to meet her friend Edith Macoy. She is a radio technician of DYKB, and a radio broadcaster in the compound. We go into her office; I love what she does.

She plays all these taped commercials after every program and gives the newscast. Janet introduces me to her, and we both watch her while she is doing her work. We just wait until she finishes her shift. The three of us go to their cafeteria and order something to drink. She is a very nice lady to talk to and very gentle in her ways. She passed the board exam for a radio telephone operator.

Janet and Edith and I become close friends as the years go by, so sometimes before she starts her shift, she drops by our house and just watches what we do for our living. She likes what we work on, especially printed curtains and quilted bedcovers. She says if she had some extra money, she would let us make her bedcover at home. She likes Ninfa, and she tells her, "I wish I was like you—very smart and so talented and because only rich people can afford to buy these to beautify their homes.

Three months have passed and the results of our board exams are released. We find out that Janet and I didn't pass the exam, so we are sad, but not worried. It's not the end of the world; there is another one after a year but not in Bacolod City. It is in Ilo-Ilo province, so Janet and I talk about that in advance. Because all her family comes from there, she still have some relatives there, and we are planning to stay with them when the time comes.

One week before we travel to Ilo-Ilo, I ask Ninfa about my exam. I need some money for my expenses, and she says not to worry about it. I always accompany her when she is looking for customers. Most of the time, we have to go first by the department store where she buys the materials, and mostly she gets the phone numbers of the people who have been looking for her. If not, we walk through the subdivision to see if we can find a new building or houses or a commercial building, and we approach the owner.

I talk to Edith to find out if she could ask her company if I could apprentice for her job, to see if I am allowed to apply for an apprenticeship. She tells me that she will try to ask her boss. Since I am always at the radio station in the afternoons when we are not busy at work, I have a chance to meet the big boss in the station. I introduce myself, and I ask him if he would allow me to apprentice for Edith's work. tell him that I studied to be radio telephone operator but that I'm waiting to take a board exam. He tells me that I have to ask Edith to find out if she will allow me. I am so glad for his response because Edith and I have already talked about it.

So, our plan is on. I don't have to go in every day while she is on schedule; I go only if I am not helping Ninfa and Rosenda at home and if we don't have a rush delivery of our work. So that's goes on until I am ready to take my second exam. This time, we have to travel far. We have to take a ferryboat to get to that province, so I am excited and this is the first time that I have gone somewhere far away.

I am ready to take my exam again, so I prepare everything. I contact Janet to find out how much money I will need to give to her relative where we will stay. She says not to worry; she will take care of it, but I have to have some amount of money with me for my share just in case. Janet and I travel there two days in advance of the day of our exam. We take a ferryboat, and it takes forty-five minutes to reach there. People are so nice—they are very helpful and kind. Janet's relatives live right in the downtown, just walking distance to the school where the exam is to be given.

So, no worries for us to walk. We have time to wander around the city, and she introduces me to more of her relatives who live a little farther from the one where we are going to stay. I like this place! It's just like in Bacolod City; people are so friendly and very accommodating. They will offer you anything to eat, whatever they have, and they have lots of fruit trees in their back yards.

The day of our exam arrives, and we are prepared. This time, Janet and I are in the same classroom but seated far from each other. I feel so relaxed this time. Maybe because I have experienced this before, any fear is gone. I am sure I will pass this time. The attending examiner is a lady who is very nice. She helps us feel at ease. It's so easy for me to answer the questions and much faster than the last time. Everyone is so attentive to their exams. The room is so quiet, and the number of attendees is not as much, compared to the exams given in Bacolod City last time. So, the day passes by, and I am so relieved that the exam is over; I can go back to my normal life again.

We are very thankful to Janet's relatives, and we give them some money for our stay. We say goodbye and we are on our way back home to Negros Occidental. Janet is back to her job in the assembly plant, and I am back to my mountain of work.

I am still going to my apprenticeship with Edith at the radio station. In Ninfa's house, where I stay, we are getting much too crowded because another two of her brothers are staying there for the school year. We are all getting along fine, and life must go on. Everyone has their own schedule— what they need to do to help out—and it seems working well.

I am trying to find my own customers so that I have some money of my own that I can give to my father at home. And I get one; a distant relative of mine who would like me to make curtains for about five small windows in her house. I go to her house to take the measurements, and I compute how much yardage of the materials we need. We look for a very light material that is easy for me to handle because this is the first time that I will do all the work myself if I can manage it. Ninfa is okay with this because she wants me to learn also. I am able to finish the curtain, and I deliver it to her house. She is very pleased with my work.

Ninfa and I are in the store buying material for one of her customers when I see a lady who is so familiar. When I get close to her, she is the lady who give us the exam in the Ilo Ilo.

So, I approach her, and introduce myself to her. She says that she recognized me and I introduce Ninfa to her. I tell her that we make curtains for the offices, bedcovers and seat covers, and she tells us that she is working in Bacolod City For the Bureau of Communication. I ask her for her name and phone number so I can contact her about the results of our board exam when it's released. She gives it to me, so I thank her and say bye.

Janet, although she is very busy at her job, always makes some time so we can get together with Edith. We go to the mall and have a good time. We share our expenses, and so we enjoy our company together. There are times when Edith invites us to come to her house, it's not far from downtown—about five minutes on the jeepney so, we go to the beach to have a swim. One time when it's my turn to invite both of them to my hometown, we also go for swimming, and they really like eating young coconut. So, my younger brother climbs up the coconut tree to get one.

Time passes by. While I am waiting for the result of my board exam, I have another idea that pops into my mind. I want to apply for an apprenticeship at the telecommunication bureau. So, on that morning, I just go into the office and ask for the name of Mrs. Dolores-the lady who gave us our exam in Ilo Ilo. She is on duty, but they have so many customers making long-distance calls from province to province, that I must wait for a while. I notice what five of the ladies are doing in the operator's machine. It is so amazing to look at them pulling one cord and plugging it into the next connection, and the ladies are so quick in doing them.

It is Mrs. Dolores break time when I get hold of her, but I mention to her what I am up to. She tells me to come back in two days because it's her day off. So I go home. Her family have a two-bedroom place at the back of and adjoining the telecom station. According to her, she has been working there for ten years already, and she is the head of the operation there. Her husband also works in the town, but it's far away and he just comes home once a month. They have two children, and her sister Elizabeth lives with them. In two days, I go back, and she says that our exams will be released by next month. She promises to look for my name on the passing list; I thank her for that and I say, "Please do." Then I tell her about my plan in seeing her and ask if she could accommodate me if I apply for an apprenticeship. She say why not, if I am really willing. I tell her that I will come to the station every afternoon at five o'clock, and she says that she will arrange for the operator, whoever it is, who is on that hour to work with me until the end of their shift. I agree.

Before I go home, I go to Edith Macoy to tell her that I will end my training with her and I explain why. At home, I tell Ninfa about my schedule, and she agrees with me. She is happy that I am trying my best to learn what I studied for; her sister and brothers are so proud of me. Most of the weekends, Ninfa's parents stay with us, so we are getting more and more crowded. Her business is getting bigger and she tells me that she's planning to buy a lot, if she can find one, to build a house on, and I tell her it is a great idea. Her family are depending on her for all the school expenses and when the parents to bring it home from their visit.

As for me, I have to get along with everyone and render the help that I can for I need her now more than ever so I can continue my apprenticeship and find a job of my own some day. The day has come for the result of my exams. I read the newspaper, and my name is on the list of first-class telephone operator who have passed. I look for my friend Janet Bautista but I can't find her name. I phone her after work, and I tell her that our exam results are already in the newspaper. I also tell her that I can't find her name, so she looks for that on her own.

I am so happy with my accomplishment now that I get the fruits of my hard labor and my struggle to go to school. But it's not complete until I find a job. I am already six months on the telecom where I'm training, and there are times when an operator takes a week off and they put me on duty. On the payroll it's the operator's name, but they give me their week's salary, which I don't mind. It's a big help with my expenses. There are time when Dolores asks me if I know who I'm talking to on the radio. It's the superintendent of the Telecommunication Bureau of the whole Negros Occidental and Oriental. I am surprised that I am already talking to the big people. I am really hoping that I can become a permanent worker here, but the number of jobs here is so limited and the operators who work here have families to feed. So, I don't think they will leave because this is government employment.

FINDING "ME"

That doesn't bother me because I know that if this place is for me, it will find the way. I am still an apprentice, but I never get tired of working here. The more I do the work, the more I love doing it. Lots of people come here to do their long distance calls because the charge is not too expensive compared to the private ones. You can meet all kinds of people here, and that's what I love about this kind of work.

Ninfa is able to purchase a lot and she is planning to build a house not far from where we live right now. Almost all her family are here now because even her mother and father, who before just came on the weekends, now they stay for weeks. It's so much more crowded now. In the nighttime, it looks like sardines are sleeping on the floor.

The job is getting more and more busy now, even Rosenda is complaining about how her back aches and that she can hardly get up from the sewing machine. There is so much rush to finish that I have to stay to help her instead of going out with Ninfa, meeting the customers and buying the materials. One morning, I get a call from my cousin Elena and she asks me if I am coming home because it is Good Friday. I say maybe, but I have to pass by the church on my way home. She tells me to pass by my sister Rosalinda's little store because she hasn't any help and with so many people coming to town for church services, my sister is so busy. I say that I will and I hang up the phone. It's eight in the morning, and I prepare myself to go, but there was a very strong earthquake the night before, and I feel dizzy due to lack of sleep. And so I go to the church in the city to attend Mass, then I catch the jeepney to head to my sister's place.

I stand by the corner of the building. It is Good Friday in my country, that day is part of the long Holy week celebration for all the churches. One jeepney arrives, but I do not move from where I am standing. Almost five minutes pass, and the owner asks if I am waiting for someone. I say no, so he says go up now, so we can go. It's okay, I'll wait for another one. It feels like something in my gut is telling me to not to ride on that jeepney. More people come and almost twenty minutes pass. The jeepney owner says, "Come on, lady. Come up now. Let's go. We're all waiting for you so we can go home." I force myself to get in the jeepney, but we travel not even fifteen minutes and the jeepney turns around abruptly and flips over, into deepest ditch of the road. Everyone is crying and moaning in pain. I am covered with blood. My long hair is soaked in blood; you can imagine how I look covered with blood. When we are in the hospital, the people ask me if there is a tape recording that can play my voice back to me. Someone tells me that I was asking her if I still have my nose.

I feel nothing in my body. I can't see my face because there is no mirror in the hospital where I am. Someone tells me that I am in a panic mood; I am looking for my knees and purse. My family hears the news, and my sister Rosalinda and my father rush to the hospital. My father has nothing on his feet when he arrives. Later on, my sister Gloria comes. They think that I will not survive. They have to cut my long hair because it's soaked in my own blood. I lose lots of blood, so much that the doctor and the nurses have to give me more blood. My eyes have been damaged by the metal of the jeepney, and I have a deep cut by the bridge of my nose. It is lucky that the inside of my right eye was not hit; otherwise, I would have become blind.

I stay in the hospital for twenty-three days and Ninfa and her sisters Elena and Rosenda visit me in the hospital. But Ninfa is there every day for a few hours to bring me some food that I like. I recover fast, and when the doctor says that I can go home, I am so happy to gather up all my things. My sister Gloria and Ninfa pick me up from the hospital and I decide to go home to our house with my brother and sisters.

I stay home and my cuts and bruises are getting better. I have to keep in touch with the owner of the jeepney because they are processing the group insurance claim, and I have to submit all my hospital records and the report from the doctor. By now, I look much much better, and I can go back and forth to their office for my claim. They say that, according to their assessment, the amount that they can give me is only 900,00 pesos because my case is not so serious, If I claim more, then I have to get a lawyer to handle my case. I don't want to get involved in this lengthy and expensive process, so I agree to what they are giving me.

At this time, my sister Flordeliza has traveled to and is working in Hong Kong. She doesn't know anything about what happened to me, and I don't tell her.

I get a letter from her in which she says she wants me to stay home and take care of my father and brother. She promises me that she will send me money out of her salary every month. I am settled at home, and I don't know what the future holds, so I just take one day at a time; I am not worried or anything. Two weeks pass and I get another letter from her, telling me that her employer is looking for someone to work with her because Flordeliza's focus is only on the two kids. I make a call to her, asking her to ask her employer to sponsor me, instead of getting other people that she won't get along with. But Flordeliza insists that I have to look after our father. I explain to her that if I am there with her, both of us can help and it's not too heavy on her pocketbook. She is so quiet on the other line. What is happening to me now is the dark night of the soul. I have been so busy all my life that I totally forgot my own self. All my life, what I have done is to help others and my family. All that is happening gives me the chance to stand back and figure out what I have done is all about my promise to my mother—to keep what I said and honor my word even without her present.

I will be twenty-nine years old soon, and I have never felt so empty in my life. Now that I am not busy and have all of my time, all my thoughts reflect on all those years that have gone by. Whatever the next page of my journey and I don't have any idea what it might be, but I never feel worry or fear in my life for I always have a means to do something.

Weeks pass by while I recover. My nose is still swollen, but I am going back and forth, processing the insurance for the accident. Soon enough, I receive a letter from the agency in Manila to advise me that I have to process my papers—I have a job waiting for me in Hong Kong. I know my sister listened to me at last. Still, I don't tell her what happened to me for I know if I will tell her, she will not get me for sure.

So, you see my dear younger brothers and sisters who happen to have had this book reach your hands and read my messages, what are you worried about and fearful about? You are not in charge (I am, me). Feel me inside of you and wake up to the truth that I am always there waiting for you to recognize me, that I am you—your Higher Self, your Higher Intelligence. It is me who does all these things for you, guiding you to do all that you do, that you have the experience and lessons to prepare yourself, so that you will not forget me, the (I am) in you, but you do not know me.

I get the money from the insurance, and I get all my papers that I need to go to Manila to process my passport. Ninfa and I have a friend in the store where we always buy the material; we know that she has a sister who works in a drugstore in Manila, so I talk to her to see if I can stay with her sister while I am processing my paperwork in Manila and if the sister could guide me to the agency that sent me the letter. She contacts her sister Nilda to say that I am coming. Nelida asks me if she can send something to her sister, would I carry it with me, and I say no problem. Monday, I am scheduled to take a ferry going to Manila. It will take about one day and one night to reach Manila. Nilda is waiting for me on the pier; I could not miss her because she looks very similar to her sister Nelida. I am so happy that she able to accommodate me at her place, and she told her landlady that I am her cousin who is staying for a few weeks until I process all the papers that I need, then I will go to in Hong Kong soon.

During a day off, Nilda and I take the jeepney and go to the market area where the agency is. We find it easily for Makati is the center of business area. I give all the requirements that they ask me for and I am so happy that I have everything. On the day we go to the Health department, I have all the requirements that they need. The lady at the agency tells me how lucky I am that I didn't have to look for a job, but the job looked for me. I just smile; I don't want to let her know everything.

On way home, Nilda and I roam around the city, just to window shop and to show me where to go when she is at work, and I am by myself at home. We go to the restaurant for our dinner that day because we are too lazy to cook. There are so many things to see here in Manila. It's no wonder that all the young ones want to travel to this big city.

This is the first time I have been here, and I don't know how to speak the language, but Nilda and I speak the same dialect.

Days pass by; I am just waiting for the call from the agency, just in case they need me to sign more paper, so I wait. Nilda tells me that, if I don't want to cook, there is a small eatery by the central market where she goes, and I can just add what I want to her list; so, I do that. After a week, I call my sister Flordeliza in Hong Kong. and I tell her that I am in Manila processing my visa to travel. She tells me to give her my address in Manila so she can send me some money for my expenses, and I am so glad that she offers me that because my money has almost run out.

In Manila, everything is new to me. People here are not sleeping as they go in and out of the house. I wonder what they are doing. The landlady has three children—one adult, one sixteen-year-old, and one fourteen-year-old. In a room that is adjacent to us, you can notice that they go in and out of the room nonstop. According to Nilda, their father is in his late sixties. They are the second-marriage children – that's why they are much, much younger.

The next morning, I am not planning to go anywhere, so I gather Nilda's laundry and mine and do the washing. At around noontime, the mailman arrives, and I get a letter telling me that I have to pick up the money at the bank from my sister in Hong Kong.. Also, I am to meet her employers at the Manila International Hotel because they arrived three days ago. Since the weather has been rainy all the time, when I go to the hotel, according to the front desk, they have already checked out. So, I didn't meet them. Every day, I go by the agency to find out the status of my papers, and they advise me that it will take two to three months to process.

I give some money to Nilda to pay our food bill ,and I tell her that I have to go back home because, according to the agency, I have to wait for three months. They say they will send me a notice when it comes, so I am very happy for that. I write back to my sister about how much longer I have to wait, and I say that I might be home in Bacolod City when she receives my letter. The next day, I go to the pier to buy my ticket for the ferry to go back home.

Most of the time, I have to stay with my sister Rosalinda in her little store so I can help her; I come home to our house just because her place has no room for two to sleep. My father and my younger brother are both doing well; they have their daily life in order and get their food every day. The fish pond is still working, and my sister gives them some money and buys them rice for their consumption. My brother is in high school now; its tuition is free because it is a public school and just walking distance from us, so there are not many expenses for his study.

Within the next two months, I get a notice from the agency, telling me to prepare for my flight to Hong Kong, which will be next week. I have to rush to gather everything that I need and go back to Manila the next day. I say goodbye to all my cousins and aunties and uncles, then I am gone. I will have just a few days to stay with Nilda, then I will fly to Hong Kong. This will be my first experience flying on a jumbo jet and on an international flight.

I ask myself if this is the result of my desire, which I asked the airplane when I was a little girl, that someday the airplane would bring me somewhere, and it's happening now. Is it a coincidence or what?

My dear younger brother and sisters, my dearest wherever you may be and whoever you may be, whatever stage you are in of your journey of life, if ever this message reaches you, as I am, dream your lofty dreams. Dream whatever it may be, keep it safe in your heart and guard it with all positive and happy feelings., One day, you will become a husbandry, and you will become a virgin who will have the fruitage of your beloved dream; it will be given into your own hands to see with your own eyes. I am your Higher Self, the Higher Intelligence inside of you is the real you; it will never fail to give your dream to you, for you and I am in you are one.

The day of my departure has come. It is Nilda's day off, and I am very happy that she will accompany me to the airport. My flight is at 1:00 p.m., and I am all set up. I check everything, especially my passport and everything that I need. I am so overwhelmed to think about my unknown journey, of the next stages of my life experience. Nilda and I are at the airport, and Nilda reminds me to find a job for her in Hong Kong, so she can follow me there. I assure her that I will try my very best.

It's time for me to check in, and we say goodbye to each other. I thank her for her support and kindness in accommodating me in Manila, and I tell her that I will not forget all that she has done. I board a Quantas Airlines plane and it's huge. This is the first time I have been very close to a plane, let alone be in One. It's a privilege—at least that's what I feel, and within two hours, I will be on the soil of Hong Kong.

While I am on the plane, my thoughts are not excitement, a sadness comes over me that I can't control, and I cry. I have to control my emotion because the person next to me is looking at me. But I can't help it; this is the first time I have traveled far away from home. Although I did not stay at my family's house, I visited them often, but being this far away, I can't say I will. I didn't see my younger sister Flordeliza in one year. I wonder if she will be mad at me for not telling her that I had an accident. But for now, I put that next.

While we are touching down on the ground, I feel so relaxed. I am so happy to think that I am in another country. When I get off the plane and look around, I feel like I have seen this place before, especially some of the buildings. It's so familiar to me. I see one lady, a good-looking lady holding a piece of paper with my name on it, and so I run to her. When I get close to her, she says my sister asked her to pick me up at the airport because she couldn't go out. Her employer is not home, so there is no one looking after the kids. She introduces herself to me. Her name is Ninit. I say thank-you for picking me up, and I tell her right away that it seems I have been in this place before. She smiles and says, "Really?" So, I say I feel so at ease here and so many buildings are familiar to me.

We head home—to my new place called home, a new employer, and a new environment. It's about thirty minutes from the airport, and we take a cab. When we get to our place, my sister is waiting for us at the door. They live in a twelve-storey building in a cluster of nice buildings. More buildings around it they are occupying two flat in the building. When my sister sees me, she gives me a hug and says , "You don't look like Neneng. My sister, you are so ugly. What happened?" I say that I had an accident in a jeepney last April. I explain to her that I didn't want her to know because she would not take me, and she says that's for sure, that in my situation, I am still healing.

I say, "I assure you that I can manage the job." And that's that.

We say goodbye and thank Ninit. She is my sister's friend, and she will be my friend too from now on. So, my sister takes me to her room to have some rest until nightfall. She brings me some food to eat, and she doesn't bother me until morning because she sleeps in the children's room every night. She introduces me to our employers in the morning when they get up. Mr. and Mrs. Lau Chi Hang, a younger couple in about their late thirties. The lady's name in English is Rosalind, and the husband is Alan. They are a very nice couple. The lady is so pretty, I can't hardly take my eyes off her. According to my sister, she is the singer in the nightclub when they meet with her husband now.

I have to invent another name for myself. I guess they couldn't pronounce any names, so I let them call me Nina. It's much easier and shorter for them to say. My day on the job has begun. My employer is training me to cook; although they serve small amounts, they include different kinds of viands on the table. And they serve soups, which take so much time to prepare. I don't know yet how long all in all because this time is only for breakfast. At this time, I don't yet have the list of my work schedule. When I finish in the kitchen in the morning, my sister and I finish our breakfast, and I proceed to the laundry.

So many clothes to wash because my sister can't do the washing. She is in charge mainly of the two kids. My laundry, I have to do by hand; they don't have a washing machine and a dryer. After that, I clean the second flat because they own two flats in the building. After all these tasks, it is almost lunchtime. At this time, there is not much to cook, only for me and my sister, but our employer and for the little ones who do not go to school yet, that takes a much shorter time to prepare.

After lunch, I have to get all these ingredients ready for their soup—so many things need to soak in water to soften them. I have never encountered these kinds of ingredients for making soup in my whole life until now. I am so surprised how many of them there are—around fourteen different kinds. After all of this, I have to go upstairs to gather the laundry and prepare for ironing. When I finish ironing and putting everything away in the closets and drawers, it is almost time for me to go back to the kitchen to prepare the dinner foods and much more to prepare for when everyone is at home.

At the end of my long day, I am so exhausted that I can hardly move my arms and feet. I don't know yet if there's additional work because our employer has not given me the list of all the chores that I have to do every day. We get only one day off; sometimes, I just want to stay in my room to rest until morning and ask my sister to bring me something to eat so I have enough rest that I am ready for the next day of my work.

I am getting used to my routine. Then, one morning, Rosalind comes to me in the kitchen and gives me the list of what all my works are. There are two more to do first thing in the morning: I will clean her car every morning, and that's six days a week, and

I will go to the market every other day. I'm just silent, at least for now. I have to find out how it goes. For the first day that I have to go down to clean her car, I have to set my alarm clock for 4:00 a.m. The parking is on the ground level, and although it's bright, I still feel scared because there's no one around, and if some one grabbed you, no one would help you because people are still sleeping—at least, that's my thought.

The first time I go to the market, it's more complicated for me because she has live frogs and bunch of them on the net on the grocery list. They are jumping on the net, and I feel so sad because they remind me that they were my playmates when I was a small kid. I can't kill them when I cook them. I can't do it. So, I tell my employer that I don't kill animals and she tells me not to worry, she will clean them.

This goes on for awhile, but I find that the schedule is so hectic that I can't cope. The time is too short because so much time is consumed in cooking and washing the laundry every day. I tell my sister to please not change the kids too often because it makes so much laundry and ironing. Preparing the ingredients for their soup is also so time-consuming. I know I have to do something. It's me who is doing all these things, and it's my body that feels so exhausted. Whatever will happen to me, it's me who will suffer.

The time comes that I have the courage to talk to my lady employer. I bring to her the list that she gave me and tell her that I can clean her car three times a week, not everyday, and as for going to the market, only when I don't buy the frogs so that's means every day so I say if you are not happy with that, then just give me my plane ticket; I am ready to go home. Of course, the result of this conversation is that she tells my sister, and it doesn't take long for my sister to confront me. She asks, "What is the matter with you? You make yourself higher than our employer?" I explain to her that if you don't tell these people how you feel, they will not know how much you are struggling with the load that they have given to you. They think that you can handle every assignment they can give. Where will I get the time to accomplish all these things that she wants me to do? I had to say something. I can't allow her to put more food in my mouth that I can chew, right? And so, that's what happened.

What I told our employer is what I keep doing, and I do it the best I can. In the end, we both get along nicely and we become a good team.

One year passes and my sister has to renew her contract for another year because of me. She asks me if I am alright with her traveling back home to spend her fifteen-day holiday. Our employer will pay all her expenses, and I give her all my savings from my salary to her, sending it all back home to help.

I meet so many ladies who work here, but this place is not for me—maybe it's the crowded atmosphere or the language of the Hong Kong people. While my sister is away, I don't take any day off, and I tell my employer that I'll look after the kids if she and her husband want to go out at night sometime. She likes that. She has been helping me a lot with the kids when my sister is away. At this time, I notice that she is pregnant with her third child, so I try to be as nice to her as I can be. As for me, she knows me well by now, that she can't get away with everything that she wanted me to do, and she is careful about that too.

I am counting the days until my sister is back, and I am eager to hear some news from home. I miss them very much. There are times that our friend Ninit phones me and wants to come by for a quick visit. I ask our employer if she would allow this, and she says she is welcome anytime. There are lots of places to visit here in Hong Kong. I like to go to Ocean Park where we have to take a ride in the gondola to go to the other side, and that's quite a long ride. My sister and I, with a few friends, are planning to visit Macao someday. I hope we can push them for that when my sister returns.

Fifteen days are gliding by so fast, and my sister will be back soon. I know I can't pick her up at the airport for I am very busy working at home. She can just take a cab when she arrives. The kids are closer to me than before. My sister is the one that looks after them, but for fifteen days I have been with them, and we are more acquainted now. They are not even asking when my sister will be coming back because I have slept in their room every night since my sister went away.

My sister has arrived and she brought lots and lots of goodies—my favorites from when we were still together, when we were all younger. She tells me that everyone is well, and I am so glad to hear that because I am always thinking about our father. I let my sister have a good rest until morning, and I continue looking after the kids. I do some of my chores little-by-little, but I do them everyday when one of the kids is at school and the other one is sleeping. My lady employer is so calm; she doesn't mind them at all, even when they make so much noise while they are playing. At this time, her tummy is getting bigger. The routine is back to normal the next day, and I am glad that my sister's back.

FINDING "ME"

I can concentrate on all my work that I didn't touch much when she was away, especially cleaning the second flat. On my day off in the coming week, I am preparing to meet one of the ladies I met before. Amoralita and I have been in contact on the phone and we agreed that I'll meet her in Victoria Square; that's the meeting place used most by the Filipina workers in Hong Kong.

Amoralita and I are planning to find the agency that has a contact and gives work placements in Canada. We get the name of the agency from one of my sister's friends, Bing, here. She applied many weeks ago, before she informed us. That means if she gets an employer there, she will be the first one to go. So Amoralita and I find this place, but she is hesitant to apply because she says that she doesn't like a cold country. I mention to her about Vancouver because I heard from Bing that that's where she applied.

I tell her I will sign an application, just for fun, because I don't have a plan to travel far away from my sisters. After all, I don't have any problem with my work now, and besides, our employer is having a baby pretty soon now, and we can renew our contract with them. At this time, Bing has already gotten her reply from the employer in Vancouver. For her, it took about five months to find the employer, and the processing in Hong Kong takes about one and a half months. She is the first one to go from our circle of friends. We are all in close contact to each other.

Not even a month after I sign my application, the agency calls me to come down to the office because I already have an employer in Vancouver. I am in a panic. I don't know what to say to our employer, but I have to think the situation through seriously because what I have gotten into isn't just for fun anymore. And so, I have the courage to tell her the truth. I still have a few months of my contract to finish, so one night, after cleaning the kitchen, I see them both in the living room watching TV. I take the opportunity to talk to them about what I have gotten into.

They look so surprised, and the husband says, "Why don't you like to work with us anymore?" And he says that if I travel that far, it will be very hard for me to travel back home to visit my family in the Philippines. I say that I know, but that I like to travel and to see some other places too. They both say that I must make up my own mind because you can't afford to leave your sister here. And I say that I am already sure that I need to go.

My sister and I talk, every now and then, agreeing that if things go right with my travel, she will follow me to Vancouver. So, it's all set. My present employer allows me to have my release paper, and she applies through the agency for my replacement. Within three months, I have exited from Hong Kong to go to Vancouver, British Columbia, Canada, as a landed immigrant with employment in Vancouver,.

So, you see, my young brother and sister in spiritual awakening, you have nothing to worry about or to fear. Everything will be arranged for you when the time is right. And if it is, you are not in charge, I am, it's me. I am your Higher Self, the Higher Intelligence, the real you, for you and I are one. Feel me inside of you, I am just waiting for you to recognize me and have a relationship with me and never again think that I am separated from you because that is not true; we are all one.

The traces of my reminiscence of how I got to this country, where I live now, from where I came are just like smoke in thin air. What a journey it has been! As I know now, it is not a coincidence at all because I remember how I felt the first day, as I arrived in this country. I said to myself that I have been here before. Everything I see is so familiar to me that the truth is probably that I lived here before in a past life. That must be so. I came to this country in August of 1981. I came here to work as a nanny for the family of Mr. Murray Green and Lynn Joli. They are a beautiful family, the three children are adorable; Michele is four years old, David is one and half years old, and LoriAnn is six months old. I settle with them comfortably; the family treat me like their own family. My job is to focus mainly on the three children and the house chores. I have to schedule them when the two older children are at school and the little one is with me.

For me, my time is gold. As soon as Lynn and Murray come home, I have to tell them how our day went, how the children behaved, and so on and so forth. Then, the time is mine. I have to go for my swimming lesson in the community center. As the months pass, my employer enrolls me in driving school, and I take a one-hour lesson for three nights. After that, after our dinner, either Murray or Lynn joins me in the car for half an hour every night so I can drive around. I learn more and get used to being on the street and to be comfortable driving. Most of all, I need practice to pass the driving test, and I do pass the test after a week of training. Thanks to my employer, I have another skill. The years move so quickly that I don't even notice how long I have lived with them. I am so comfortable living with them that I forget that I have my own life to work on. By then, Lynn has given me the time to take a course at the Vancouver Community College. I enroll in a long-term care course, but there's a problem. Although I finished high school and a vocational course in the Philippines, I am not qualified for the Community College because the standard of our schools in the Philippines is lacking about two years. So, the Community College doesn't accept me. I say that I can't go to high school here for two years because my time is limited—I am working. I say, "If you can, give me a written exam." I am glad they did give me the written exam; out of forty questions, I passed thirty-four, and they accept me in school.

Six months have passed so quickly, and my practicum exam is fast approaching. Lynn has to take vacation from her work, so I can attend to my practicum for fifteen days. Luckily, I passed that final exam, and I have my certificate.

My life and my hard work, I owe it all to my very best employer. Their kindness, love, and dedication to me allowed me to improve my skills so that I can apply for other lines of work.

Time passes by, and although I am ready to step into another stage of my life journey, I am skeptical that I can make it on my own, thinking about having to pay everything from house to food and every expenses. I am hesitant to leave yet. Besides, I am so attached to the three children. By then, the oldest is ten years old, the second is eight years old, and the third is six years old.

One day, I am at the bus stop when one lady gets there and we start talking. She is in her eighties; we exchange our phone numbers and that is how our friendship starts. She lives with her daughter, and her daughter has a nine-year-old daughter. I am acquainted with them for quite some time, and one day, they tell me that, if I'm ready to leave my employer, they'll rent out their one bedroom to me. I tell them that I have to think it over. When the time is right and I am ready, I will tell them.

So, one day, I tell my employer about this family I have met. She tells me that whatever my decision is, just to give them enough time to find someone that will take over my job. Although the children are big enough, they still need someone to drive them to school. The youngest one is so attached to me and she doesn't want me to go. She is always crying to her mother to not let me go. So I agree not leave for at least another year.

This is end of this chapter of my life. The new world has opened to me for next journey of my life.

If only more people would do the same as what my employer did for me, this world would become a better place to live in, and hunger would become lessened. It's because they saw the beauty inside of me were concerned about my well being, not the color of my skin, not of any religion, not of my race, and not even of my size. They felt inside of them that which loves us all.

My friend Puriza, the daughter of the lady that I met at the bus stop, offers me one bedroom in their house where I can stay. She tells me to pay the amount that I can afford for now, until I can find a job that can support me. I help them clean the house and help with cooking our food, and I do all the groceries once a week. I don't mind because I still have a little savings in the bank.

Every day, I look for and apply for jobs. One morning while I am taking a walk, I come across a Filipina lady and we talk about work. She tells me that she's working in one facility called a nursing home, a long-term care facility. I ask her if she can help me to apply where she works. She tells me to apply, and she gives me the address and her contact number. She is so friendly to me; she is in her late thirties.

I don't go there right away. I wait until at least two weeks pass. In the eighties, it's not difficult to find work, so my sight is to apply at the hospital. I make applications to so many places that whoever calls me first is where I'll go for an interview. I go to the place that this lady has given me; it's not far from where I live now, so I ask for an application form.

It's a combined intermediate and long-term patient facility with about twenty-one patients. Besides this, the nurse tells me that they need one nursing aide and that the shift is from 11:30 at night to 7:00 a.m. I have never worked those hours, so I think I want to try. I pass my application to her, but I don't really prioritize working here, so I keep applying everywhere.

One evening when we are having supper, Puriza says that she has a male friend who wants to meet me. I say that I don't have any experience meeting someone who is a male in this country. Besides I say, I am still busy finding work. So, she becomes quiet, and we don't talk about it anymore.

At this time, my sister Flordeliza, who was in Hong Kong, has already arrived here and she is working for one couple with one child who is just three months old. Since she is a midwife, she has the expertise to handle that job. During her day off, we meet in downtown, and I bring her here to the house where I live now. We are both much happier than when we were in the same house, working together in Hong Kong.

There are times when she invites me to sleep with her in her room where she works and vice versa. It is October and Puriza opens the topic again about meeting her male friend. At this time, I don't mind at all because I am not alone. At the meeting, it should be me, my sister and two of my sister friends, so there are four of us. I tell her that we want to meet him here, at her house.

She plans for the meeting to take place on Thanksgiving Day, October 11, 1984. We prepare some food so we can all celebrate the Thanksgiving Day. And my sister arrives with her two friends, one is our friend from when we were in Hong Kong, and here comes this guy; his name is Fermin. He is introduced to us by Puriza; they met during their rehabilitation from work-related injuries , so they are under the Worker's Compensation Board.

He is in his fifties, at least fifty-one years old. He is a good-looking man, about 5'5" in height as I observe. He looks like a decent person and is very respectful. After our supper, we all have a cup of tea and chat in the living room. When I get up to get something from the kitchen, he tells Puriza secretly that he likes me, at least according to her. That's our evening.

My sister says goodbye and leaves with her two friends, but I stay at home to help Puriza's mother tidy up the kitchen, and after that, Fermin and I are left alone in the living room. Once in a while, Puriza comes to chat with us, knowing each other is a good thing. He is a gentle man, and I like him too, but we need to know each other very well.

He works for the Commonwealth Construction Company as an iron worker, and according to him, he is able to work on two of the bridges here in Vancouver. He says that he arrived in Canada in his twenties. He is from Spain, so mostly his employer assigns him to jobs outside the country because this company is all around the world.

He is still on his vacation, so he comes about every other day, just to say hello. There are times when Puriza and the two us all have a little walk at Queen Elizabeth Park. It's so close to where we live and is also walking distance to the apartment where he lives. One afternoon, we stroll in downtown, and I see this beautiful high-rise, peach-colored building, and my eyes are wide open in amazement. I say to him that is the place where I am going to work., He looks at me, questioning me if I am serious, and I say, "Tomorrow morning, I'll go and apply there."

And that's what I did. First thing after my breakfast, I take a bus and go to downtown to apply to a big, new hotel in town; its name is Le Meridien Hotel, a travel companion of Air France. It will really be a dream come true if I can work here. I go to their Human Resources department where a lady named Miss Jane gives me the application form. There are two ladies who are also applying to the housekeeping department. After I am done, I give my application to her, and I go home. I couldn't stop my eyes from looking back at the building. How proud I would feel if I am able to be a part of this institution.

Days have come and gone . I have a strong feeling that I will get the job. And in exactly one week, I receive a call from my previous employer asking me if I applied to the hotel. I say yes, and she tells me that they asked her lots of questions about my performance at work, my loyalty, and so forth. She tells me that she gave them the truth about me and a very good recommendation about my skill and how easily and quickly that I learn new skills.

Three days after all of this happening, I get a call from the hotel, telling me that I will be starting to work the next day. I am so excited that it's hard for me to sleep. Morning comes, and my friends and sister are so proud of me. I am ready to start my next journey and my new lessons at work. First, I go up to the HR department, and Jane brings me down to the housekeeping department. I am quite nervous, the same as everyone feels when it's the first day on the job. I am introduced to Annith, the manager of the housekeeping department. She is a very nice lady and very helpful to me. During the briefing, it's about thirty-five ladies who are working that day, plus six housemen who do errands if our supplies upstairs on the floor run out.

I'll be working with another lady for a training period of three weeks, and I am sure at that time I will be familiar with everything—where to go to get supplies and doing all the jobs that I came to do. Anne is the name of the lady I'm working with; she is so nice and gentle to me that I relax and absorb and observe every detail of what she does. That's for a few hours of our job; after that, she asks me to give her some of the tools that we need in the rooms—that way, I'll remember where I'll get them in the closet because every floor has a closet.

Our day goes smoothly and we don't make any mistakes. Just being in this building, I am flooded with inspiration and daydreams. There are times that I am carried away by the beauty of the chandelier or the fixing light on the hallway. I feel like I am on air; it's such a beautiful feeling. It's just like magic. I have to go with Anne's days off for the three weeks that she is training me, so I can concentrate on how she does the job with speed. For this kind of work, speed is so important because fifteen rooms are not easy to finish if you are a perfectionist.

Every day, we have an additional room to do, one room for our first day so that's sixteen rooms and the second day is seventeen rooms and so on and on. Each day is not easy, but it's how we build up our speed. One week just glides by, then we are in our second week, and Anne gives me one room to do on my own; the longest we can stay in one room to finish up is thirty minutes.

When you exceed thirty minutes, it means that you're behind, so I am mindful of that. When I finish my room, I have to ask her to come and have a look so she can see how I am doing, and she makes some correction if some of my setting is not right. For my first day alone, she assigns me three rooms to do, and to tell the truth, it is really tough. But this is my choice of work, and I must do it right. So far so good, but by the time I get home, I can hardly move my arms and legs for tiredness.

I have a little time to spend chatting to Puriza and her mother at night, but I fall asleep quickly because I am exhausted at work on a daily basis. Even to my boyfriend, Fermin, I just say hello on the phone at night. And when my day off comes, I have so many things to do. I have to do my laundry, go to the grocery store for our weekly food, and help clean the house. All I can do is invite my friend Fermin to come to the house if he wants and have dinner with us.

This has to go on until I am made permanent in my job. This is so important to me, for my future and so I can keep my promises to my mother. I always honor my word because it is just who I am. Sometimes, when it's my day off, my sister drops by and she sees me working hard to clean the house. She gets so upset to see me doing that because she tells me that it's not my own house and that I shouldn't kill myself working so hard, plus no one is helping me. It's difficult for me to explain to her that it's because I am paying them $150 a month. But then, I am also buying groceries for the four of us in the house, and she doesn't agree with that.

After three months of work, I pass my probation test, so I am hired. That means I am working fulltime now. I deserved to be accepted because I work so hard. At this time, I have more acquaintances at work, and it's more fun because we can chat in the cafeteria before we start work in the morning. I am at home by now because most of my coworkers are so nice and friendly. But if that was not the case, I would have nothing to do with them because I come here to work, not to find friends. It's as simple as that.

Every month, I send money back home to my father. There are times that I have to go shopping for his clothes and send the package through the post office. In the eighties, mailing packages was not so expensive. Sometimes, I ask my sister if she can ask her employer if she can have the same day off as I do, so we can spend our time together and have an outing with her friends and mine.

I am very careful when it comes to handling my money. I have a good plan for my savings and, at this time, I increase the payment for my room. I do that because my friend Puriza and her mother don't ask me to do so. I am a very understanding and responsible person when it comes to the expenses in the house, even if it's not my own, and I feel how difficult it is to maintain a property.

I am always mindful to do my work, so that I won't lose it. Working at my shift, which is always in the daytime, is very important; it's not like working in the hospital where there are no permanent shifts. My workplace has become my second home now. I eat my breakfast at work every morning, together with my coworkers. We have to pay a certain amount for the taxes, which they take out of our paycheck, and we have a meal twice a day.

We are getting busier at work now that this hotel is so well-known, and most of the celebrities stay here. I always work on my day off if they ask me to because overtime is paid at one and half our regular pay. I have more money on my paycheck, and I am doing that almost now and then. There are many times that my coworkers ask me if I don't get tired. And I say, "I have to work hard while I am still young because, with this kind of work, you have to take the opportunity while your body is still young. It's heavy work, and I don't take my body for granted." They say that they have never thought of it that way. I say that I do, and besides, I don't have a family here, so I will use my time wisely.

I have so many plans. When I have enough savings, in my thoughts, this is the opportunity for me to keep my promise to my mother. When I was a five-year-old girl, I promised that I would help them the best I could. Although my sister is here with me, I don't expect her to help me but wait for her to offer. So far, she hasn't.

I haven't heard from Fermin for awhile. The last time we talked on the phone, he said that he was about to return to his work, and he did't know where he would be assigned. I don't really mind if we don't see each other. I'm not ready for that, and we don't have any commitment to each other. So, for me, life must indeed go on.

Puriza, my landlady, and her boyfriend have decided to settle down for she has been a single mom for quite sometime. I must decide where to begin again. During my day off, I mostly read the house or room-renting section of the paper. I don't wait for them to tell me to move because I know her boyfriend has a house in the next town, about a forty-five-minute drive away.

I find one room in the basement of a six-bedroom house. Two other ladies live in the other two rooms in the basement, so we will be sharing the living room, the kitchen, and the washroom. I don't' mind that for we are all ladies, and we can schedule our cleaning time.

Another chapter of my life's has begun. I tell Puriza that I am moving out on my day off, and she asks me whereabouts. She wants to come when I move, so I say that would be nice. They will know my whereabouts and that I am safe. She tells me that they are planning to sell the house. She wanted me to come along with them to Surrey, where they are looking for a house to buy that's much bigger than their house right now, but I say that it's too far for me to travel back and forth to work. It's alright for them.

I settle in to my new place—a new environment, new roommates, and new adjustment. The upper house is rented by one couple with two kids, and the yard has big cherry tree, which the kids hang on, but they play most of the time. The neighborhood is so quiet and safe, and I can have a morning walk if I want. I ask my sister to stay with me in my new place during her day off, but we don't have same day. However, she can come and stay.

Although my life has lots of twists and turns, I find it unique because it seems like the dots just connect so beautifully. I don't have to spend too much time figuring things out. I am just guided about what to do along the way. I received an invitation to a wedding of the daughter of my lady friend where I used to live. I am so glad that she has met someone younger than her. She is sixty-four-years-old and the guy is only forty-three-years-old, but they are really for each other. I think that it is so beautiful, that marriage is really made in heaven, which is in the hearts of two people. Age doesn't matter.

I am still doing my work beautifully and sometimes I go to work without money in my pocket but when I go home, I have something to buy groceries that I need at home, through the tips that guests give me. It's very handy, but it doesn't happen all the time; however, this kind of work allows you to make them. Sometimes, I make mistakes— I miss doing something because it is so busy and I have to do the work in a short time, like when the guest is already waiting in the hotel and the previous guest is late checking out. That almost always causes the problem, but what can you do? Things happen all the time without you expecting them to. When I am called into the office, it is not a good feeling at all, but that's how I learn a lesson on the job, not all things are gold and roses.

But I guess life goes on. We are dying and we are learning at the same time, as the saying goes. I never forget any obligation to my family, no one imposed them on me; they are of my own making, but things happen for a reason. I am still sleeping, and it's all our up bringing when we are growing up, that's how we were taught in our community and in church.

I'm walking in downtown one day, and I came across my schoolmate Rosita, and we have a little chat., I get her phone number and promise her that I will phone her on her day off and so we part. I have lived here in my place for almost one year now. I don't have any problem except for my parking spot. It's on the street, and it's difficult to find a space sometimes when you move the car, but I get by everyday.

I have been in my job for almost four years now, and I work steadily; plus, I work one day during our time off, once a week, and so my savings grows quicker. I am still in contact with my friend Fermin, but we don't have an intimate relationship because it seems we both are cautious. We want to know how we can make it to be sure. But, he is so busy in his work, and I am too; so, that's fair.

FINDING "ME"

I call Rosita, my classmate, just to say hello and to ask her about where she lives. I find out that it's not that far from where I live about five blocks away, so it's walking distance to me. I ask her if she is available if I drop by to visit her, and she says that it's alright. So, I go and see her. I am so happy to see her again; It's more than five years since we were at school.

Her place is in an apartment house that has eight suites. She lives on the second floor in a bachelor suite. It is a very nice area and a clean house, and the landlord lives opposite her in a two-bedroom suite. I ask her that if there's a vacancy someday if she will help me get a bachelor suite like hers. She says yes. She has lived here for six years now. She works in the nursing home about six blocks away, so she just walks back and forth to her work and that's a good thing.

I tell her that I wish I could invite her to my place, and we could cook some of our favorites food from back home, but because of sharing the kitchen, it's difficult for us to do that. She says not to worry that when I move there one day, we'll do that, and we laugh. So, that's that, and I walk back to my place.

Although, I spend most of my time working, more than my scheduled time, I don't mind at all because I love to work. Instead of having a double job, I would rather have overtime one day a week at my work. Some of the girls at work tease me by saying that I should give them some of my overtime days, and I answer them you better change your days off so you have one, and I laugh.

That's how I make my extra money so I am able to support myself and help my family back home. At this time, my only brother is taking a course at the Maritime Academy as a Seaman, and I am the one who supports all his expenses. Since I left home,

I have not been able to go back because my priority is to stabilize myself here in Vancouver. Not very long ago, my friend Rosita called, telling me that I should prepare because her next-door neighbor is leaving next month, and she told her landlord that she has a close friend who will occupy the place next, and that's me. I thank her, and I am so happy because, although it is a bachelor, at least I will not share the kitchen, the living room, and the washroom with anyone.

My sister is finishing her contract with her employer, and she is planning to move to the USA. She met someone during her visit there, and she has decided to get married there. I do not oppose her decision because she is already mature, and she can decide what her life is to be. Living here in a far-away city on my own now, I don't feel scared or worried at all. It seems to me that I am safer living here than living in my country where I was born. It's much easier for me to navigate my livelihood here and to live comfortably here on my own.

I receive a letter from my younger brother, asking me when I can come back because they miss me so much. It's almost eight years since I left home and I have never gone back. I explain to him that I can't go back now because I am supposed to move to another place, and I have expenses for moving, plus sending money back home every month. It's not an easy task for one to budget my expenses.

At work, life is much busier than ever because the hotel is very well known in the city now. It is always full of tourists from all over the world. Most of our long stays are the movie stars like Pierce Brosnan He stayed with us for four months. They were working on one movie in Vancouver and during that time, I am assigned to the twenty-first floor, where the presidential suite is. I am eager to see this very famous guy, but the movie people mostly leave so early that I couldn't catch him. I say to myself, there must be one day that I'll meet him in person.

And that one day happens, but not in a nice way. When my supervisor pages me that the guest has phoned downstairs to say that his room is ready to clean, I am doing one of the occupied rooms, and I can't leave the room until it's done. By the time I get to his room and knock on his door, he is in the living room and, before I open my mouth to say that I'm sorry for being late and to explain what had happened, he is so upset and says, I phoned awhile ago. Why did you not come right away? I introduce myself to him, telling him that my name is Inocencia and that I am assigned to keep his room for your initial stay with us. I say that I am very sorry for being so late, but that when he phoned, I had just started an occupied room, which I can't leave until it's done. He says to me, "go on," then he left. But after a few seconds, he came back to me and handed me a one-hundred-dollar bill. That's how I know a person has a heart.

It's not easy to work for the whole day after having to encounter such unhappy face. I learn my lesson, and hopefully, it won't happen again. I didn't tell any of my coworkers about what happened that day, and when some lady asks if I have met him, I just say that I haven't seen him yet. Sure, I lied. But who wants to talk about a sad story, having to face an unhappy encounter with such a very well-known and beautiful human being inside and out. I kept it to myself until now.

After four months, when he left, he wrote me a short letter, telling me that I could have all his leftover things that he could not take home, and he gave me an envelope with five hundred dollars in it. I share it with the girls who turned down his bed at nighttime.

So, you see my younger brother and sister in spiritual awakening, just say something and acknowledge your mistakes. Don't be afraid, don't be so worried, and don't fear for anything. If you share your courage, you'll know that it's not you, your personal self who is talking on doing any job but the real you, your Higher Self, the Higher Intelligence inside of you, you and he are one. If you believe in God, believe also in me. By believing in yourself, everything is possible.

I am living in my new place now, a place where I can afford to live, at least for now. Although it is a small space, I have everything that I need for myself, a kitchen where I can cook my food and a washroom that I can call my own and no one to share.

I am very thankful to my friend Rosita for helping me to find and move into this place. For now, I tell myself that I can settle here for a little longer time. My commute to the bus is very handy for the bus stop is just in front of the building where I live. The backyard is a big open space with apple trees and pear trees, which are full of blossoms now, and I can smell the sweet aroma of the flowers. I like it very much. Rosita's days off are Tuesdays and Wednesdays and mine are Wednesdays and Thursdays, so we have one day together when we can go to the park if we want. She loves dancing, and she always goes dancing with her friends. It's the opposite for me because I don't know how to dance, so I can't go with her.

When her two nieces come for a visit, Rosita cooks and I do the same, and we all enjoy the food in my place because mine has a little more space than hers. That's how we can share in our new place, and I have more fun now than before.

At work, life goes on. There are no changes from my routine, and I am used to working hard everyday plus my one-day of overtime. That's steady during summertime because we are so busy. Out of the blue, Fermin gives me a call; we have not communicated for at least eight months now because he was back at work. He just came home the other night. He was assigned to work in the interior of British Columbia, and he stayed in the camp until the job was done.

I am so proud to tell him that I have a new place now and that I don't have to share with anyone, although it's a bachelor suite only. He says that he is sorry that he didn't call me for such a very long period of time, and I say that I am used to that and besides, I am busy with my life too. With that, we hang up the phone.

My friend Rosita tells me that she is starting to look for her own place to buy, a one-bedroom apartment because the prices, at this time, are affordable. I ask her if I can go along with her sometimes when she is looking for one. She says that she has already a prospect. She phoned the owner, and she is going to see it on her day off, Tuesday. I am working, so I can't go with her. I am so proud of her. She is being so responsible, dealing with life in a way that I admire so much. I say to myself that I will do the same someday.

These are the kind of people that I want to be surrounded with. They don't play around with their time and money; they put it to good use. Unlike most of my coworkers who always go on outings and going to restaurants every weekend. That's not my lifestyle anyway. I don't tell anyone at work what's going on in my life. Unlike them. When they come back to work, during our time in the cafeteria before we start our work, they always discuss what they do during the week. That lifestyle is a no no for me. That is why, when they sometimes ask me to go with them during our day off, I say that I can't for I have only one day. They say you can give up sometimes, and I say, but I like it that way.

One day, I have a call from Puriza's mother , she tells me that she wants to come to live with me because she prefers to be with me than with her own daughter. But I say that she can visit and stay at least a week, but she cannot live with me. I can't allow her to be alone by herself when I am working. If I allow her and something happened to her in my place, how could I face her daughter. After all, the mother is in her eighties, what a disaster it could be for me.

Back home, although I send them my help every month, they always ask me when I can go home for a visit. I can't tell them when because I have so many plans. They say that my Father always asks them to write to me, asking me to come home. I tell them to tell him to relax and wait because I am working hard for that.

I am so careful dealing with all the people at work, but I am in trouble now and then, when I could not stand to listen to our manager doing our briefing. She does it in the morning before we start our work, and she does it again—every time we come down after our day. Hearing very hurtful words every day with no one even answering back bothered me, and one day I couldn't stand it any longer. I reacted and said, "Excuse me, but do you think what you are doing to us is right? Is it proper for you to do that when you have an office to call us to privately when we make a mistake.

If I am the one who made a mistake, call me there in private." She asks me if I don't like that? And I say, "who does?"

The girls say, "Inocencia, you are our hero, but always remember, the hero dies first."

I reply that "I am nobody's hero, but say something to make a difference. No one will know her mistakes if no one opens their mouth to correct it."

I know I risk my job in doing that, but that's the right thing to do. so just say something have a courage for no one can have put down you.

Some of the girls keep a distance from me now that they know what I am capable of, but I don't mind at all. I know that I do the right thing for the good of everybody. That's all that matters. After that happens, our boss never does it again. But every day, there's always somebody being called into her office, and I like that. At least, she does it professionally. She learned her lesson at last.

After a long day at work, instead of cooking my supper, I stretch my back on my bed and fall asleep for a few minutes. When the phone rings, it is Fermin who just wants to say hello. But I was carried away in my conversation to him about my work, until he mentions something about an investment. He says to me if you have some money, you can invest in these two companies, and he gives me the names. I am thinking that I have some savings, so, why not? But I am new to this idea. That's when we hung up the phone, but this tip about investing is in my thoughts for the whole day at work.

On my day off, I go to my bank and withdraw a large amount of my savings. When the teller asks me what I will do with the money, I tell her that I will invest in the stock market, and she asks if I have an advisor, I say no, and she says that she hopes I do well with my money. I thank her for that. I go to the Stock Exchange House and open an account and invest in the two companies that Fermin mentioned to me. I just check the stock exchange on the television, and I don't worry about it.

My life goes on with my new times every day. I feel so comfortable where I live now, that no other people to get along with and to deal with. I just pay my bills, and life is so beautiful. At work, there are ups and down, but I can deal with that. No worries.

My next-door neighbor, Rosita is moving out in two months, and she is doing her window shopping during her days off. I say to her that I am going to help her with her move, and she is happy about that.

At the end of every year, we always get a pay raise. It helps me to quickly accumulate savings because I pay only a small amount for my accommodation. Since it is not a one-bedroom apartment, it helps me save more. I am so fortunate to have a job that I really like. It's hard work, but good pay. I like this job; so, it's easy for me to deal with it and that helps because I don't feel tired at all, even though I work six days most weeks, and that makes a big difference.

During the slow season, we do our general cleaning at the hotel; it's scheduled for three months, so we work two people to a room for three rooms each day and for five days. We clean from top to bottom, and everything inside the room is fixed and changed. That's how our workplace is well maintained when it comes to cleanliness. I highly recommend the Sutton Place Hotel.

Today is my day off, and Rosita my next-door neighbor has decided to take some of the lighter packages to her new place. The previous owner has already moved out, so I tell her that I will come along to help her. Her new place is a one-bedroom apartment and is much roomier compared to the new buildings nowadays. This must have been built quite some time ago.

She is waiting for some new things that she bought from the store to be delivered; it's not difficult for her because it should be delivered right to her new place. I can imagine how it feels to have your own place. What a privilege to own one. Someday, I will feel that myself, what a freedom to feel. She keeps taking things little-by-little until the end of the month, and it's very handy for her.

I am thinking that I have a new neighbor coming, and I do hope we become friends too. Rosita is farther away, and we will get in touch, but it's not like when we are here and can be together anytime we like. Life is beautiful—full of surprises! You don't know what will happen. At every turn, there is something new, and all we can do is hope for the best and do what ever we can, to observe, learn, and experience; that's life.

I hear from my landlord that my new neighbor will be two young ladies who live together, and they both work at the nearby hospital. I think they could be my friends, if they want to. But it's okay with me if they don't. I don't want to bother anyone; it's just a thought.

I phone my broker about the investment that I made almost six months ago, and the result is not bad at all. I am glad to know that because it is much, much better interest compared to when you put money in a savings account at the bank. But, for now, I don't touch it, but I will sure keep an eye on it. Fermin and I didn't have time to spent together, even for just a little walk around like we did before I am so busy with my work, and he is as well. This time he told me on the phone that his coming assignment will be in Northwest Territories. That's quite far away, and he doesn't know when his job there will done; sometimes, he's gone for months, sometimes for years. It's very difficult for him to say when he will be back. There are times when he has paid for his apartment for one year without living there. I think it's a waste of money, but that's his life—always away. That's the way his job is.

Our friendship is steady as it is. I don't expect more than that because it's in the air. Besides, I have so many dreams to realize back home. Although I am by myself here, living here in Vancouver, I can't decide if I want to live here forever. All I know for now is to take advantage of my work, save more and make the best of my life here.

I don't plan for my future, and I am not worried or fearful at all about what might happen to me without anyone to help me. All I know is today. I don't worry about tomorrow; I admire that kind of attitude. I take one day at a time.

Rosita has moved to her new place, and I am able to meet my new neighbors. They are two Filipina girls in their twenties, and they are nice girls—very jolly and respectful people. I just hope that we will get along because neighbors are my family here in this far-away country. Even though Puriza and her family treat me as one of their family, they now live far away from me.

I have to make some adjustment to my routines during summer because the days are so much longer. When I come home from work, after my suppertime, I go walking for about half an hour, just enough that I get tired, which makes it easy for me to fall asleep quickly. Then, I don't think about Rosita my neighbor; otherwise, I feel sad. There are times that I go swimming, and it's much better for my sleep.ok

I am used to being by myself, and I like it that way because I can focus on what I want to do next, and if some changes come along, I can plan my future for myself. I don't have any plans to visit home yet, but I don't neglect my monthly support of them. I have a budget for that, and I am very careful not to exceed that amount.

There's a lady at work who is new, so I am always friendly to her so that she will feel at ease with our company. I really know how she feels being new to the job. So, during our break time, I go to the floor where she works, and we go together. Her name is Greta. She is kind of shy and is a very secretive lady; we're kind of similar in character, and I like that. We're not too open, and we don't engage in gossip.

She lives with another lady's friend, and according to her, they were classmates in high school back home. She becomes my close friend at work.

There are times when she finishes earlier than me, and she drops by to help me finish my rooms, then we can go together for a short break in the cafeteria. We share stories of our childhood, and we laugh about everything we did as children. We were so carefree and didn't have a care for in the future. But her life is much better than mine because she was only one when her father passed away; later, her mother got married again and she has a half brother.

She grew up with a very strict father because he is soldier, and she was not allowed to have many friends. That's the reason why she is very quiet and shy to approach and mingle with people. She tells me that Candy, her friend, and she are planning to buy a place of their own. I believe her because they both are working in the hotel, and Candy has worked in a Vancouver hotel for a number of years now and has some savings.

I listen to her very attentively, and I want to apply what I hear to my own life someday. That's how I learn to improve my life and set my goals. I don't like being in the company of friend who just talk about what they do on their weekends—going here and there just for fun and outings without any direction for their future. I am not attracted to that kind of storytelling, that is why my friends are carefully selected.

One morning, she tells me that there is a new hotel at the waterfront that will be built very soon. It is a sister company of the Hotel Vancouver. She is planning to apply and she asks me if I want to move. I say that it will take time to build a building like that, and I say we will see, but, in my mind, I don't have any plan for that. I have been in this place much much longer than she has been, and I am already established here. I have become one of the trainers for newcomers here, so why would I cause so much hassle for myself by moving somewhere else. It doesn't make sense to me—just my thoughts.

Life must go on no matter what. Time for me as important as gold; that is the reason why I traveled halfway around the world—to make as much as I can for my opportunity in life and that I wouldn't make at home, not only for myself, but for my family back home.

Every Thanksgiving at work, the company gives us a whole turkey of about ten pounds. Since I am by myself and my friend

FINDING "ME"

Rosita has moved, it's time for me to visit my previous employer, the one before the Green family, and give them the turkey. It's really nice to see them all again; the children are all in University and are grown up now, but they never have forgotten me. They are as respectful to me now as when they are younger.

My employers are so proud of me. They say that they were right in their recommendation that they gave to the hotel where I work now. We have a little chat, , then I depart for home.

I am so happy where I live now. It really doesn't matter if I live here several more years. The landlord has raised the rent since I moved here, and that's three years ago. He is a very considerate person because he was a working man all his life until he bought this property after he retired. That is also why my friend Rosita could save and buy her own place. That's what's in my mind to do while I live here, to save as much as I can. I keep an eye on my investment and, so far, so good, but I am not ready to sell it yet.

And that's why younger brother and sister in spiritual awakening, you don't have to be a genius, a very smart person, or a special character to change your life for the better. You just need a little organized thinking, an open mind, listen to the people around you (even in the public you can hear people talking about what they do), observe your surrounding to see the good things, and apply it all to your life. You will be surprised how your living conditions improve. I don't follow their extravagance for I know I cannot afford that, at least for now. Just open your eyes and ears wide to catch the good things, but not the bad ones.

Each one of us has a built-in intelligence inside of us that saves us and guides us in how to navigate to live and to survive in this beautiful planet of ours called Earth. So what are you worried about? It's all about the "I am" in you! It's "me" who is in charge of you.

It is almost the end of the year 1992, and I check with my broker about my investment. The news is really very good, and I want to sell it out. I want to let my friend Fermin know and hear his opinion, so I give him a call—after all, it was his tips that made me decide to invest. Luckily, he had just come home from his work far away. He asks me how I feel. And I say yes! So, he says to go ahead. I call my broker to sell my stocks, and I am so glad that I did because what a harvest!. I have a fat savings account in my bank now and what a smile on my face every day. No one knows at work because I don't talk about my private life to anyone except to my close friend Fermin.

At work, they are starting to decorate the outside surroundings for the Christmas Holidays. During this time, we always have a Christmas party in our department, so our boss' assistant starts selling the raffles ticket for fifty-fifty draw. I buy fifteen dollars worth of tickets. After work, I go window shopping. This Christmas, I want to dress up a little extravagantly. After all, I am the only one who knows how much I have in my bank account now, and I have a big smile on my face while I am thinking.

The inspiration that I feel now is because of my courage, my choices, and the actions I have taken. It gives me more courage to do have bigger dreams. I am thinking of buying my own place, like Rosita and Greta, my friends. I like what they accomplished in their lives, and I'd like to have something to show for my hard work too, so I can see it with my own eyes, and I can touch it with my hands; that's what I want.

FINDING "ME"

Christmas is here at last, and I feel so excited. I have my beautiful dress that I bought the other day in a small Chinese boutique not far from my home. It's not so fancy, but classy and really looks good on me. I think, I'll surprise my coworkers because they haven't seen me in a good-looking dress. We have the choice to contribute money for the meal or we can bring food that we can all enjoy for the party; everyone is so excited.

Since we are the biggest department in the company, most of the other departments drop by and enjoy the food that we serve. Every year, that's what they do. It comes time for our raffles. This time, our boss announces that because she collected more money this year than last year, there will be six draws, and she begins the first draw. Everyone is clapping their hands, and when she reads the number, it's my ticket. The prize is seventy-nine dollars. She starts for the second draws, and when the number announced, I check another ticket and, luckily, it's mine again. This time, many others are clapping their hands and instantly are looking at me like who is helping her have all the good luck! But it has happened before; some houseman won twice last year, so it's common and my prize is one hundred dollars. I am so happy for these wins. Some girls are saying how lucky I am, but that I don't need that because I always have lots of tips. Someone else says, it's in her personality. This time, I hear our manager and assistant manager mix the numbers very well, and she draws again for the third time. When she reads the number, guess what? It's my number again, and our manager quickly throws all his tickets that he is holding into the floor. He shouldn't have done that. It's not my fault. They are the ones doing all the draws. I don't know what's happening to

79

me, but hey! They're my wins, not my problem, and on that night, I gather two hundred and seventy-nine dollars.

And that's the reason why, my younger brother and sisters in spiritual awakening, that I say that it is already within us—all the tools that we need to survive in this beautiful planet we call Earth. So why worry? There's nothing to be feared. We all have a guidance, have our instinct—the gut feeling about what to do and not what to do. It's automatic and teaches us that we all have it, so it's up to us how to use it, right?

We have all the Higher Intelligence within us. It's up to us to find and have a connection to it and to know that higher power, instead of a separation from your Higher Self. You will be amazed at the result of being one.

The bus that I take everyday to work passes the area where I see a construction sign for a new building, a thirty-one-story residential building to be built within two and a half years. I like the area because it's right in the heart of the city, and it's close to the Waterfront. It is along the corner of Hasting and West Pender streets.

As soon as I come home from work, I give Fermin a call, asking him if he has been in Downtown lately and if he has seen that sign. He says, no, so I tell him to go and see if he likes the area, and he says, yes, he will.

I hang up the phone and start to prepare my supper, so I can go to bed early. It is more tiring to do general cleaning in wintertime than doing our regular schedules because, although we clean only three rooms and two of us work together, there are more things to do, plus the smell of the chemicals makes me sick and dizzy, and my skin gets very itchy, and I get rashes.

FINDING "ME"

The next week, at the end of my work, I go looking for the showroom for this building that is about to be built. It is in one of the rooms at the Holiday Inn Hotel, so I go in. Someone mistakenly shows me the layouts of each suite for this building and the price ranges. One of the layouts on the twentieth floor catches my attention because of its perfect squares, which I like. I know I can afford the price if I have to wait for another two and a half years. I can save more, and I will have more then enough money for the deposit before it is finished.

I go home and phone Fermin to find out if he was able to see the area, and he says yes, and he likes the place. I explain to him every detail that I got at the showroom, and he tells me to pick one that I like, and whatever I like, he will agree with me.

He asks me if I want to go up a little bit higher. But I say that the prices are much higher. He likes the thirtieth floor, but I say it's too expensive, and he agrees with me. On that day, he comes to my place and gives me the check for a good amount of money, and the next day, I go back and put a down payment on that suite.

At this time, I didn't touch the money that I gained from my investment. I will save it just in case they ask for an additional amount for the deposit; I am always thinking ahead.

After a couple of weeks, the building's realtor phones me, asking for an additional amount of money to put down, so I was right in my thinking. When I go and give them the check, they tell me that that's the last payment until the building is finished. When we move in, we will pay the total amount, and I am so glad for that;, I have more time to save, and there is still a big amount in my savings, so I don't have to worry.

It's back to normal at work; it's the same routine everyday. It's always busy, as usual, but I'm not new to that; after all, I have been working here almost six years. After all, I save more here compared to my job before, so where else I would go? Patience is what I need now that I have started a new project—not a small one, but a big responsibility.

During the nineties, I feel the urge to begin what's been in my mind to do, the reason why I decided to come to this country in the first place. Now that my brother is graduated from his course, I have to save for something else that I will do later. For now, I am supplying money for their food and especially for my father's medicine ., It's not a big amount because the exchange rate at this time is quite high, and that helps me a lot .

Way back in 1989, was the first time that could go home to see everyone. Ten years had passed before I was able to go home and, at that time, my father still needs me and was still looking after his fish pond. At that time, he was in his early seventies, and he would ask me to sponsor him so he could come with me. I told him that he'd feel homesick because he'd be alone at home every day because I work every day. He says that he just wanted to see what Canada is like.

I love my father very much, but I can't see him lonely here, so in my mind, I won't do that. But I just say to him, I'll work on that.

In the early nineties, I receive a call from my brother, telling me that our father is not feeling well and that they brought him to the hospital. He has high blood pressure and is low in potassium, and I have to send some money for their expenses.

I do everything not to panic and tell myself to just calm down. I can easily do that, no one would notice what's going on in my world. I am very good at hiding my emotions.

I perform well at work; I can't afford to lose my livelihood with the kind of condition, I'm in now. I am in control, and everything goes as smoothly as it can. I will handle everything that life gives me, whether good or bad, I'll handle it.

In April of 1992, my brother phones me again. If it's possible, I have to go home. Our father is not in good shape, so I have to plan. I call my sister about what's going on, and I ask her if she can come along. I still have my holiday vacation at work , so I apply to take it right away. I tell Fermin about my plan, and the next day, he comes to my place to give me some money to use.

I am able to go home, and I am so sad to see our father. He had lost lots of weight. He could still manage to go around, but he is very weak and needs someone to hold on. He is very happy to see us—my sister together with her five-year-old daughter, Rosalie, and me. My father still reminds me that he wants to come with me when I go back to Canada. I say that he must try to get better, and I will work on it. Deep inside of me, I know things are not so bright for him.

I give him a bath every day and make some jokes that make him laugh. It's good to see his face brighter and everyone laughs. I am good at cheering them up. When he is resting in his bed, I lie down beside him and talk about my job and my life in Canada. I ask his permission to get married soon, and he asks me to bring my boyfriend home, so he can see him. I tell him that he works far away from me.

He tells me that it's alright because I am old already, that it's getting too late if I want children. I say to him and everybody that my life in Vancouver is boring and no fun, but just work and home. I am trying to discourage him from thinking about coming with me, when I come back.

I ask him what he wants to eat because I'm going to the market, and I will buy what he wants me to buy him. He wants some rum, and I say that's not good for him. It's too strong, and you get nothing from that. But he says he has missed it for a long time, so I buy one bottle for him. I say just a small amount every time he wants to drink. My goodness, I can see his face lighten up for that drink alone. It's really the truth that he missed it so badly.

I take care of him every day that I spend with him. I cook his food, feeding him every meal. He really likes that he's just like a baby again. I have to go to the market every morning to buy fresh fish and vegetables and different kinds of fruits that he has never eaten in his life because they're so expensive, and they could not afford to buy them.

Every morning, I bring my father for a little walk in the morning sun before I give him a quick bath. It's really a good feeling to take care of my parents, but I never experienced it with my mother because I was living in the city, working for the money for their expenses, when she was not feeling well.

I wish I could stay longer to care for my father; the days are passing so fast, and pretty soon, I will be leaving for Canada. I remind my father that soon I'll be going back to Vancouver, and he says, "Will you bring me there?" I tell him to get well first and eat more, so that he will gain back his weight, and we will go from there. And he smiles at me.

FINDING "ME"

A few days before my departure, I gather all my siblings that live close by, and we talk about the our father's situation, of whatever it might become, they might need to take him to the hospital if something wrong happens to him. I leave a good amount of money with my sister Rosalinda because she is the one who lives in my father's house, where we all grew up, and she is the one taking care of him.

I try to be as happy as possible, but inside, I am dying; I am so aware that I am leaving all my family with this situation of my father, but what else could I do? After all, they depend on me for all the expenses, that's how tough their lives here are. It seems like things have not improved since I left this place. People's lives here are much tougher than when I grew up here.

Most of the land that belonged to our distant relatives is now owned by a family that I have never known. I feel so strange in this place that I called home before.

Maybe it's because I have been away for so many years now, and the surroundings have changed a lot, but I could not recognize what and where before. I don't have much time to explore for I want to spend all my time taking care of our father. I have noticed that even though he has a good appetite, my father never seems to gain weight. I make him feel happy and as comfortable as he can be, so that he will not remember the discomfort of his sickness.

Every day, he has visitors who come by to say hello to him, but most of them, I don't know. Maybe I met them when I was here before, and they asked my father, who I am. Is she your daughter? I have not seen her here. And my father tells them that I live abroad, and they tell me how lucky I am.

The day has come for my departure, and I assure my father that if he gets well soon, I will work for his papers to come to Canada, and I can see the smile on his face. I try so hard to keep my emotion from showing in my face, the sadness that I feel inside me, and I say goodbye to everyone. My father cries, but he still remembers to remind me to leave him some money to spent in case he goes to the hospital, and I say yes, for your food and medicine too.

I leave with a heavy heart, not only for my father, but for everyone who lives here. The toughness of their everyday lives is not easy. At least, that's how I feel, but you can't see that in their faces. It seems they are used to it, and they always smile.

My flight home goes smoothly, and I get home safe and sound after fourteen hours travel in the air. I am so exhausted from my trip that I just go and lie flat on my bed.

I call them the next morning, and I talk to my father. He sounds happy, and I feel at ease. My sister and her daughter left one day ahead of me, so I am sure they are at home by now too.

That's how tough my situation is. Sometimes, expenses just come all at once, if I didn't have savings, how could I manage all of these? I have to live with that—that the person who has been given much, must give. This is the law of life that every grown-up must know.

I have one day more to spend at home before I go back to work, and I am supposed to take advantage of getting more sleep to recover from my flight. I prepare my food early on, so if I feel hungry when I wake up, I don't have to bother cooking. Usually, I put in earplugs when I sleep during the day, so I won't hear any noise, although this place is quiet. But sometimes, the people passing along on the street are noisy, especially the children coming home from school.

I go to sleep around 9:00 a.m., and I get up at 5:00 p.m., and I don't feel hungry at all. I force myself to do something, so I will not over sleep. Otherwise, I won't sleep at night, and it will be worse because it's my first day back on the job. It would be so awkward for me to be tired, but I don't know what to do first.

I go out for a walk just to refresh myself. It is summer, after all, and how good it is to feel the gentle breeze of summer that makes my skin a little cooler. How nice to be back in Vancouver at last. The beautiful, blooming flowers on the different kinds of trees along the streets are so good to see. I am carried away by the wonderful scenery—I suppose ten-minutes walk has become an hour long when I look at my wrist watch. I race home so I can have my supper and go back to sleep to be ready for my first day at work tomorrow.

I am so excited to think about everyone at work. I can almost imagine how excited they will be to get some news from the Philippines, especially the girls who are from my province. They always want to know what's going on at home.

I make a small bowl of vegetable salad and toasted bread for my quick dinner, and I prepare all the things that I'm going to bring to work tomorrow, especially some delicacies that I brought from home to share in the cafeteria. I clean myself and go off to bed. I'm surprised how easily I fall asleep because I have been sleeping all day. I'm sure it's a lack of sleep, plus the tiredness from traveling.

Back to work; at least, I am on my usual schedule at the bus stop, 6:00 a.m. I have the same bus driver, and he notices me. He says to me, you must have been on your holiday for I missed you for quite some time. I say yes. This is my first day back to work. Back to reality, he says with a smile, and I laugh.

A few of my coworkers are already in the cafeteria when I come, and I get one large plate to put all the goodies that I brought back from the Philippines. Most of the girls do that when they travel, and we are like a family at work.

I tell the girls to enjoy and they are so pleased to try. I ask them if there is anything new on the job that I have to know, and they say no, it's your routine. The first day at work is just like the first day at grade school —the pumping heart, the nervousness; it's an awful feeling.

We all go downstairs to prepare our stuff for work, but I go to the washroom just in the hallway leading from our department before doing that, but on my way back before I pass the short staircase from the second floor, a big tall guy collapses right in front of me. His cup of coffee scatter all over the place.

I shout as loud as I can so someone in my department will hear me and call security quickly. I don't want to touch the person for security reasons. Not even a minute passes before the security person comes; after him, lots of people come to help, so I leave to get ready for my shift. I explain to my boss what happened to this guy for the report. How lucky I am that I was not right in his way.

I concentrate on what I'm doing, trying to forget what happened this morning, to make my day go as smoothly as I can, so I don't forget anything in the room that I am cleaning. It must be as spotless as I can make it so I have no complaints from my supervisor later on.

When I am on my way to the closet to get some items that I need in my room that I'm doing, one of my guests in 2101 tells me that she had a hard time sleeping last night because her bed is so soft and she has a backache. I tell her not to worry, that I'll do something for her tonight. I ask her if she is ready for me to clean her room. And she says that she will be out in ten minutes, so I keep an eye out for that, and she thanks me and leaves.

Before I clean her room, I phone downstairs for the houseman to put a bed board under the mattress in that room. Sometimes, it takes awhile for the houseman to do all the requests because he has to cover five floors. Each houseman works eight hours a day, and we have four housemen working in the whole building every day.

What inspired me to work this kind of job is not every day is a hard day. There are times that the guests don't touch anything in their room, including this lady's room. She didn't touch one thing, especially in her washroom, and that makes my day lighter. But there are other rooms that it seems were ruined by the storm! As I said to the guest, I fix her bed. I hope she will have a good night sleep tonight.

I end my first day back at work nicely after all the happenings that started this morning. Since the sun is so bright and still up high when I get off work, I decide to walk home, instead of taking bus. I have two ways to reach home. I can either cross the Granville Bridge or the Cambie Bridge. I take Cambie because it is a much shorter walk, and lots of people are doing the same, walking just to enjoy the pleasant evening. Plus, the beauty of nature along the way is worth the effort.

I reach home. It takes me half an hour; I sure wonder if it will help me to have a good-night's sleep tonight. The nicest thing about living alone is the feeling of freedom, which I enjoy very much, and I am really used to. You don't need to consult anyone, whatever decision you make. It's not that I am not an easy person to get along with, but I just don't want to share my place with any friend or coworkers like most of them do at work., I can pay my rent by myself, and I think it's better to be independent. That way, I learn to be a more responsible person.

Next morning at work when I see my paper, I have an eleven o'clock checkout, and I know it will be a hard day not only for me, but for everyone. It seems like you can hardly breathe because, just about every five minutes, the supervisor is paging me to rush cleaning the room because the guest are already waiting. Most of the time when it's like this, I skip my morning break at 10:15, just to save time in finishing the room I'm in.

Today, the guest that I was servicing yesterday, whose bed I fixed, is looking for me, but she couldn't see me in the hallway. Instead, she saw the houseman, and he tells me that the guest in 2101 is looking for me. So, I go and knock on her door and she is there. She tells me that she is checking out today and she is waiting for me to come by because she couldn't go out of this building without telling me how happy she is for my help with her bed. She slept like a baby last night, and she hands in me a brown envelope. I thank her and she tells me that she gave a note to the front desk to give to the housekeeping department. She adds that I am a treasured asset to this company, and I say thank- you again and leave.

FINDING "ME"

My eyes twinkle all day. I didn't tell my coworkers, but what a good feeling when someone recognizes your hard work. It gives me more inspiration to make my work better. That's the reason my boss made me one of the trainers for this job.

I don't have an easy day today, but I make it. That's all that matters. Not all days are like that because most of my guest here on the twenty-first floor are long-term guests, for mostly, they are movie stars. Every two years, we have a raffle. The floor you pick is where you'll be assigned for the whole two years. This time, I pick the same floor, that's why I have been assigned here for a longer time.

Days, weeks, month have passed by. I don't hear from Fermin or from home. I'm hoping that all things are alright. Today after work, I plan to pass by the site where the high-rise building is being built. My future living place is about five blocks to walk from my work. I'm just hoping that my day will be easy today, so I will not get behind.

Ups and down are always to be expected at this kind of job, but I can manage that kind of happening because we have to learn from our mistakes. We don't have to put that into our hearts or else life is unmanageable. So far, my day is peaceful, no complaints from the guests or from my coworkers. So, life is easy and beautiful.

My way home passes by the site. I am bombarded by all kinds of happy thoughts and imaginations about how it will feel to live in a twenty-floor building. How will it feel living in the downtown area with all amenities close by? The Waterfront is outside my window. The church is just a five-minute walk away. I ask myself: What else could I ask for in life? It's just like heaven on earth, isn't it? How simple and easy life is, if you make the right choices and follow up with action and coordination. Everything will just fall into place.

On the site, the work is progressing now, and the whole area is surrounded by fences. That means there will be no more cancellations for the construction, and I'm so happy for that. I decide to continue walking until I reach home, crossing the Cambie Bridge again with the beauty of the setting sun in the horizon. I always find that the beauty of nature inspires me as I live by myself in this far-away land.

When I arrive home, I meet the two young ladies, my next door neighbour. We chat a little bit, then we head back upstairs to our rooms. I prepare my supper and go to bed early, walking home makes me more tired and sleepier for sure. When I get up in the morning at my waking-up time, I am well rested, and I have lots of energy to burn for my day at work again.

The month of June is here again, and I always send some money to each of my sisters to help them out with the school expenses for my nieces and nephews. They are so happy for that help. It is my inner knowing that I send them help without them asking me, when they need my help. After all, this is still a part of my promise to my mother that I gave a very long time ago, and I always keep that. For me, it's a way to maintain my wealth and to keep more and more coming to me.

My life continues to prosper. There is never a day that my pocket is empty when I go home from work day. The guests really appreciate the work and when they are happy with the job you do in their room, they are generous. Cleanliness and neatness are always my focus when I do my job.

Some girls who work on my floor have complained to me, saying that they are more tired when they work on my floor, compared to when they work on other floors. I asked them why, and they said that I tuck in the bed sheet so well that it's hard for them to remove it at one corner and pull it out. I asked them if they got tips from my floor. They said no, and so I said that's because they do a sloppy job. No wonder why. Some girls tell me that they like to work on my floor because they don't do much cleaning because there's nothing much to clean. I maintain my cleaning, so I don't have to do much scrubbing.

When I do my work, I do it as if it is my own place because, for one thing, it will add up to my life and my experience.

I care about the company that employs me, and that's supposed to be because honesty is the best policy for both parties; that's how it is, at least, for me. For others, it's up to them. I have my own standard and ethics to follow.

I don't have much happening in my social life except that sometimes, during the long weekends, I do go camping with some of my old friends who I met when I was new in Canada. Some of them don't have any family yet; we get together and go for a long drive to Okanagan where we can pick lots of fruit like cherries, peaches, and blueberries. During that time, we pay only twenty-five cents a pound, so we always bring lots of fruit home. It's really lots of fun doing that. But as the time goes by, most of them get married and have families. That pulls us apart in the long run because our contact has gone. Now, I can't trace some of them anymore.

But that's normal when it comes to friends or human connections. When the times comes that we lose contact, it should mean that both sides have been around for each other; there's nothing to be sad about, that's what life is. Nothing lasts forever. We have to enjoy here and now, for tomorrow is uncertain!

On June 23, 1992, my brother phones me, telling me that our Father has just passed away. I feel sad, but I have already prepared to accept his passing because when I was home, I witnessed his suffering, and I didn't want him to suffer too long. I decide not to go home to attend his funeral for I was there a month ago. Instead, I send more money for their expenses.

My boss gives me three days off for my mourning and reflection, but before that, she asks me if I am going home. In that case, she could give me an extra day of vacation, but I say no, to that was that. My father was seventy-eight years old. I lost my friend and my beloved father, but life has no guarantee. The day we are born and the day when we go are not in our keeping.

We must all just accept the way it is because it is what it is, and it's beyond our control. We must not dwell on the sadness because it can paralyze us, but each one of us has different ways of dealing with the reality of life. That's normal; you have to deal with it in your own way, and that's healthy.

After my mourning, I get back up on my own two feet. What else can I do? I am alone here, and I depend on and trust myself. After all, what else would we want? If we know what is within us, we could just get deeper inside our being, and every guidance that we need would just pop up to help us do what we need to, so each one of us is all the master and teacherare. What else we are worried, fearful, or sad about? We all are one and capable of creating what we want our life to be; you have no one to blame but yourself by not waking up to your truth.

FINDING "ME"

Wake up, my younger brother and sister. Look around you; the beauty and richness of the earth is limitless and inexhaustible. Open your eyes and claim your royal inheritance for no one will do it for you; we are all royalty in this beautiful earth of ours. Don't be shy because, if you have the courage to do, all kinds of magical doors will just start opening for you. What are you waiting for?

The high-rise where I bought a one-bedroom suite on the twentieth floor is already standing tall, and my happiness and inspiration flood me. I feel so proud of how much I can accomplish if only I put my focus and desire of what I want to happen in my life.

I give Fermin a call to see if he is already home, but there is no answer. That means he is not home yet. I just keep myself busy; my main focus is always on how to make more money, and it seems like magic attracts money to me. I buy a lottery ticket, and when I check it, I win $3000.00. It so happened that one of my co-worker's is there in the store on that Saturday, and she says that I am so lucky. Even at work, she says, I always have tips. On the next Wednesday, I win again, but only $1,200.00. One of the Chinese ladies at work says to me that there's one more win because our belief is that if you win a lottery, it should be three times in a row. So there's one more win coming, and she was right because the next Saturday, I got one more—but for only $400.00. I can tell now that money attracts money; it's been proven to me many times now.

And sure, those winnings are going into my bank account. I am making more money now than five years ago because my salary increases every year. For me, life is so easy. Whatever I want to buy, I can have it, and although my job is a manual one, I don't struggle at all. I feel happy and light. All I know is I can do it; I believe in me.

Months pass into years, and 1996 comes. It's the year of the completion of the high-rise building, but our closing is not until July. Then the company will turn the key over to me for moving in. I'm a little anxious about what to do if Fermin is not home from his job, but I think—it's only January. I focus on my work to easy my mind. Days go by, and my routine is well established, and that's a good thing.

I know my life is not balanced for I work most of the time. No play is not healthy, but I am an adult now, and I am different. I am a responsible human being, and I honor my word all the time. When I say I will do something, then I will do it. I always find the time to make it for honesty is the best policy. Whatever the outcome on my projects, whether good or for ill, no one will harvest it but me and me alone. So I am always careful for what I wish for, so I am able to make it. That's so important to me.

There are times in the cafeteria at work that the ladies, my coworkers, open the topic about why I never tell them about my life. What do I do with my money? What are my projects? So, I just say that there's nothing to tell. They know I help my siblings back home, that's all. What else do I do? "I am alone here," I say.

I really avoid talking about my personal life at work because of how easily the stories can become a gossip; it's like wildfire. That's why I keep it all to myself—whatever I'm planning to do in the future.

My work is sailing smoothly, no trouble that I cause and no one has brought trouble to me, and that's good. So far, our manager has changed like five times since I started to work here, but for me, I am still standing; that's how tough I am when it comes to earning my living.

I always think that in order to live a good life, you should built a solid foundation first; that's why I don't mix work with pleasure. I work with all my heart to have a steady life for my future. I am so serious about my savings and where to invest so I can make more, hoping that my savings will last for my lifetime.

So, you see, my younger brothers and sisters in spiritual awakening, each one of us has our own time line to grow up. But, is the knowledge not in our inner being all along? Can we get all our knowledge from our inner self—knowing what to do, knowing how to escape hunger and to have a better future? And where else can we get more clarity than from our own light of which we all partake. We are all connected to one another, part of love and life, in that we are not separated from one another and everything that is; I'm that we are all one.

Today is my day off, and I'm thinking that after I do all my chores, I'll give Fermin a call to see if he is back home. The building is getting closer and closer to its completion, but whatever happens, I have no concern because I have savings in the bank, ready for that, and it's in my name.

But I have to consult with him because we are in this together. So, I give him a call, and luckily enough, he arrived just last night. I ask him if he could come to my place so we can talk a little more deeply about our plan and investment; I mean this property.

So, we talk about our future and where it is going. Do we have to plan to live together? He says that when the new place is completed, we will move in together. He has decided not to accept assignments that are far away anymore, and I like that. After all, we have known each other for ten years now, but we really don't know each other because we have always been far from each other because of his work, and I am always working too.

He tells me that he is planning to go home to visit his siblings in Spain. He still has one sister, three brothers and six nephews and nieces there, and he wants to visit them. I am so happy for that. According to him, he hasn't seen them for quite sometime now; so I say it's time now. I don't ask him how long he is going to stay. I am used to that; after all, we are always far from each other and we don't have any commitment to each other yet. This is fine because, to me, freedom is important to each of us.

So he is away again, and I don't know when or if he will be back again. I know he will not give me a phone call if he is traveling, and I am used to that too. Time passes and my work continues. I have peace and calmness in my own company, and I'm fine with this. My life has been that way for a very long time.

I contact my sister in Florida, and we talk about life—hers and mine. She has a family now, but me, I'm still on my own and we laugh. She asks me about Fermin, and I say he is in Spain right now, and she ask me why I didn't go with him, and I ask her for what? I am working, and she just gets quiet. We talk about her daughter Rosalie, and she says that she grows so fast. I tell her that one day, when we settle down, I'll visit them, and we hang up the phone.

My comfort is my work place. This is the place that I came to It is so comfortable for me to be here; it is my second home. These two places are how my dreams turned into reality, and I'm sure many, many more dreams will be realized.

Today is my day off, and I have to go for my groceries. I don't buy much food for the house because, most of the time, I eat at work. So, I run out for just some vegetables. I don't need to take a bus; I can just walk ten minutes, and there's a grocery store where I can buy every thing I need.

I go in the entrance and am surprised. It's already the middle of the day, but I see very few people inside. All I see is a cashier with a man standing in front of her. They are talking, but the lady looks so pale. She is looking at me. The man has a piece of paper that he hands to her and he has a big knife in his hand. It seems that the lady is pretending that she can't understand English, and the man tells me come over there so I can tell her what he is telling her. All I do is look at him like I'm going to eat him. I pass by and rush to the back, where so many people are buying things. I tell the owner that the cashier at the front is being held up, and I get out quickly through the back door. I don't know what happened after I left. Sometimes, strange things happen that you don't expect, but my instincts are always alert, telling me what to do, and that's good.

Instead, I take the bus going to downtown and go to another grocery and get what I need and come home. I keep myself busy, doing my little bit of housecleaning and my laundry. Then I have my small lunch and a little nap. That's how I spend my one day off. Monday morning comes, for me it's the start of working six days in a row. For some, it looks so boring, but for me, it's like a holiday because I love to work, especially when I receive my fat pay check. It makes me more inspired for living.

A month has passed, and Fermin comes home; he brings me a few pieces of jewelry, and I can tell that he has a good taste through his choices. I thank him and ask how his family is doing. He says they're alright; he is not good in giving details; maybe he doesn't like doing this, so I don't ask for more.

He tells me that he will be home for awhile—until they call him onto a job. But he will not travel for his assignment; he will not accept it. And we talk about the closure of our new place, and we don't need to wait for long now, I say.

I won't do much overtime, at least for a while, because I want to spend time with Fermin. I want to know him more and to find out if we can get along together. I am thinking about our future, about living with someone. I know it's a big adjustment for both of us because we have both lived alone for a very long time. Freedom is so important to us.

The developer of the building has already contacted me to be ready with the money. They will hand over the keys to the owners of the individual suites very soon. They also give me instructions about which bank they are dealing with in case owners can't afford to pay in full cash.

I am so excited! Very soon I will be living in a new building, on the twentieth floor in a high-rise? I think it's heaven on Earth. I'm just hoping that everything turns out right. Although all the suites in the new buildings nowadays are not as big as those in the buildings built long ago, it's good enough that I have one to call my own.

The manager of the bank talked to me about how large a mortgage I have to apply for, and I said that I'm not sure yet. I have to check my bank savings account. I tell Fermin that very soon I'll go to the bank to see how much is in my savings account for the developer's closure of the building, then he will give me another check to add some more. So far, we have a good amount to pay and I can apply for a smaller mortgage at the bank.

When I bought the suite, Fermin told me to put it only in my name. The developer's lawyer asks if he should add my boyfriend's name to the title of the property, and he tells me that by this time, I have to share fifty percent of the property with Fermin. I say, yes, I will because he is my partner, and that was that.

On July 27, 1996, we go to the bank and settle everything and sign the land title. So, that's it! We have the key in our hands. We are so proud of our accomplishment, and how proud we are to be going in and out of a building right in the heart of the downtown area. We like the layout of our suite; it is a perfect square—both living room and bedroom. We are satisfied with everything; from the kitchen and the washroom, the view is breathtaking—facing the ocean and mountains of North Vancouver, and on the living room side, we the view Metrotown and the whole of Burnaby and City Hall. It is worth the money we spent.

Fermin has to move in just because I want to move at the end of July. We are able to buy a few things more beside. I don't want to bring my old stuff to our new place, so everything must be new. I put most of my stuff in a garage sale, although I didn't make much from them, but at least I don't have to carry them. This is the end of my living by myself.

New life, new adjustment, living with someone. I don't know how a big gamble this is, but I have to start somewhere. Life is always like that with lots of surprises that you wouldn't think of, but I am always prepared for the unknown ahead. I'm always ready for that. My motto is to go forward, not backward.

Our life so far is good. We get along most of the time. We arrange everything; one of my pay checks goes directly to the mortgage, and Fermin has to pay for the utilities and our food expenses. I have to spend more for the maintenance, but that's fine; it's only my tips from work.

So you see, my younger brothers and sisters in spiritual awakening, all the knowledge that we learn is within us , and we apply it to how we deal with our life. The choices that we all make, the actions that we take, and the kind of life that we all want to live, the knowledge is about what we must do in order to live happily and peacefully and to escape hunger is all inside us. ? How simple it is, and yet it's so difficult for many, especially when our minds are cluttered with so many thoughts and worries, fear, anxiety, and sadness that we can't find a little quiet to listen to the voice of the one inside us. It's trying so hard to tell us what to do, our true self, the one and only is always there to guide us, to teach us. It is our only master and teacher who always has the patience to wait for us to connect and recognize him. Yet, we don't have eyes to see and no time to listen; that's the reason why we have a difficult life.

It's time to reveal my story to Fermin about why I traveled halfway around the world, stopping in Hong Kong for a few years, and landing in Vancouver, Canada, to follow my dreams. I followed this path because I promised my mother to look after the family, and, although she is no longer here on this beautiful planet of ours, I am loyal to that promise. I tell him that my words are my life and keeping my promise is my honor and my legacy.

He understands me, but he asks if I don't think it is a big work for us to do. I say that we won't do it now, but at least he knows; it will be the next project after we finish paying the mortgage, and he says, "Oh! I see." I try so hard to put aside much savings, so when the time comes, there's money to start my next project. Once I say it, I am sure I'll do it and see it with my own two eyes, that's how determined I am.

Four years goes by. I finish paying for our place, so that means my expenses are now only for the maintenance, and that's a small amount. By 2002, I am able to visit them at home. I stay for a month, and I am able to talk to an architect to draw up a plan of the house that's in my mind. It's a small, three-bedroom house, twenty by twenty square meters up and down with a long staircase. The two bedrooms are upstairs and the house has an attic roof style with a small balcony. After two days, he shows it to me and I like it. He gives me a blueprint.

It's built on a piece of property that belonged to my father, it takes about a year. The next year, I go home again and finish everything—painting in and out, buying furnitures and beds for every room, and that's done.

So, I plan for another house. This one's not so big, but it has two small bedrooms and is build of solid concrete. It is for my sister Rosalinda, and it's built by all my nephews and cousins. I don't spend so much on this house, compared to the other one, and that's fine. My sister and her husband are responsible for buying their beds and furniture, and that's a big help to me.

And now, I'm preparing for my brother's house. He and his wife have a picture of the house that they want to copy—the style and the paint outside. My nephews sometimes work for a construction company; they tell me that they know lots about the work because they have been constructions workers for so many years. One of the people they know is their foreman, who is available; he knows all about construction, and he has steady people who is working with him.

I want to meet him, and I phone. He comes to meet me. I'm so lucky because, at this time, they have just finished the job that they were working on. He has ten people, and my brother shows him the picture of the house to be built. He says that he can build it with his people, and he asks me when he can start. He says to me, if you want, we are ready to start working now. We talk about the daily pay of his nine people, about his daily pay, which is much higher than the others, and the pay for individual specialists. Their pay depends on the line of work that they have mastered.

And the work begins. It's being built on my brother and his wife's lot . It's been donated by the government in an area for all the people who live there. It's about one hundred square meters, so it's not a big size. The house will be up and down, one bedroom on the lower floor and three bedrooms upstairs.

In our country, we can apply for a house construction permit at the city hall at the same time that we begin the work, so we don't have to wait for the application to be approved. I get all of the material that I have to buy at the city hardware store, and because it's not that far, about half an hour travel, the hardware company can deliver all the material that I buy. That's the start of the biggest project that I have committed myself to do, and I intend to finish it.

My one month holiday is almost over, and I have to travel home soon. I give instructions to my brother that I am going to send the money to finish up his house. The construction of the building is already halfway done, and I like the work that they have done so far—solid and good finish work, not sloppy. They are very organized and don't misuse the materials. They are very economical in using them with not too much waste cutting the materials, cables, and wood.

I tell my brother that the money that I will send is for the house budget will be—for the house and the salary of the workers. Otherwise, his house will not be finished, and he says that he will do all that I say.

While I am doing the project for my brother's house, I give a small amount of money to his wife Lilian to start up a small store where she can sell all kinds of things that the workers can buy. Then they don't have to go somewhere else, wasting their time. And my brother is raising pigs, which helps a lot with their living expenses and with the children's expenses at their school.

When the workers finish on that day, I call them all, and we have a little chat. I tell them that I am going home, but that my brother is in charge of them. They have to continue until it's done.

I tell them that they have to respect my brother, like they respect me when I am dealing with them. I say that it is my good intention for everyone of them to get along in the job without any accidents, and that when I come back, we will see each other to have a little gathering. Everything will be taken care of off their salaries and whatever materials for the job. They just ask my brother. I caution them that there are to be no abuses of work.

At the end of every workday, I always buy some drinks for every one of them to enjoy before they head home. That's so they can share with one another and to talk about their work for the next day. I ask the guy who is in charge to tell me all the materials that I have to buy before I go home. I ask him to estimate the material so they can continue working for at least a week after I'm gone. If he gives me the list, I can buy it all now. My brother and I go to the hardware store and buy everything that they need for the job to continue after I am gone home.

I give the rest of the money to my brother, the budget for their food everyday and the workers' salaries for one week. I have counted everything already, and I tell him not to touch it for his own expenses because I'll be very upset if he does. He promises not to do that. And that's it, the next morning, I fly home to Vancouver.

I arrive home without feeling exhaustion at all; it seems like nothing has happened even after all the responsibility of building my brother's house and controlling the ten people who are working on the building. How did I manage that? Everyone got along so that the project was done smoothly. No accident happened, which is good, because there's no insurance for them. I know what happened there, when the intention is for the goodness of everyone, the universe does the rest.

Fermin did alright while I was away for a month, and I am back to work after a couple of days resting at home after my long flight. I am so lucky to be able to work in this place, especially the work I do. It makes a big difference that I can do the work that I love. I never feel tired; I enjoy going to work every day and without any complaint after so many years. I can't say how long I'm going to do this kind of work because it depends on my body—how it handles the stress and manual labour. So far, this work has sustained all my accomplishments. I explain to Fermin that the house that I am building for my brother is half done, and I have to send them money once a week to finish it up. It's so lucky that, at this time, the exchange rate of Canadian dollars to Philippine peso is quite good. They send me the picture of the progress of their work, and I am so happy at the outcome. It's to my satisfaction. Fermin is happy with the design of the house too.

We get along nicely with the project. And I know, deep in my heart, that this is the last project I will do because I have to prepare for my own retirement. I am not young anymore, and I'm with Fermin. It's not fair that I help my family so much because he seldom sends help to his sister and brothers, and I know that is why I have to stop somehow.

I am surprised that he never complains to me about what I am doing, that I focus on helping my siblings more than ourselves. But , I have to keep my promise to my mother. My oldest sister, Gloria, two of her kids are going to school with our help. One is taking a teacher's course in the university; the other one is becoming a heavy equipment mechanic. I tell them that one day, they have to look for a job and help the other sisters or brothers and not to start their own family until they can help each other, then the others will help another one when they finish and have a job.

Our help started with four of my siblings; we also help two kids to go to university; each one of them must help the other when the time comes and they get a job someday. I just hope that my good intentions for each one of them will be realized someday in their future. I do my best to help them because I am the one who has been given the opportunity to do so, and I do hope that someday all of them have an easy life and recognize our help to them.

You can see, my younger brother and sister in spiritual awakening, all that I am doing. It's my choice to help, no one has forced me to help; no one has forced me to do so except myself. Because of my selfless love for them, I acted without feeling sacrifices and tiredness. I know that no one will understand what I am doing, but it's done smoothly, so it is what it is, I guess. Sometimes things happen without our knowing. There must be some Higher Intelligence inside of each one of us all, and I know someday he will reveal all to us. I have my inner knowledge that my instinct is guiding me in doing all this because, in my ordinary personality, I can't do all these things. And they're done well. I can't think that my ordinary self has done all these things all along.

Every two weeks, I send money to my brother to finish up his house, and he sends me pictures of the work's progress, and I'm happy with it. I always remind him to tell the working people to be careful in their jobs and not to have an accident because that's the worst thing that could happen.

Fermin tells me that he feels that something in his stomach is not right, and he says that he has felt this for quite sometime now. So, I ask if he can manage to see the doctor, or should I stay away from work today. He says he will go by himself, so I go to work that day, but my job's not easy today because I'm thinking of him and thinking of all the bad things that can happen.

When I come home, he tells me that he went through all kinds of examinations and had an X-ray to find out why his stomach is bothering him . He says that tomorrow the doctor has scheduled him for a quick surgery. He doesn't explain to me what kind of sickness he has in his stomach.

I phone onto work, saying that I can't come in tomorrow because of an emergency, and that's fine. They can always replace me. We go to the UBC General Hospital because that's where the specialist for this kind of surgery is always on. This hospital is a little way away from where we live. I never feel nervous or fear or panic, but while Fermin is in the recovery room, I tell him that I have to go to work to ask my manager for an extended holiday to stay home to take care of him.

Although I have just come home from the Philippines after a month's vacation, I still have three weeks of holiday time from the accumulation of holidays that I have never taken, so I take fifteen days off to stay home with Fermin. We stay in the hospital for one week. I stay with him during the day, but he asks me to go home at night so that I can rest. Besides, I do nothing much for him because, most of the time, he is sleeping, and the nurses are the ones looking after the patients.

One week's gone and we are about to go home. The doctor tells me to give Fermin something to eat fairly often, but not too much because almost half of his stomach has been taken out. He never explains to me how serious the disease is. Each time I feed him, he throws it up all; he can't hold food in his stomach. And he tells me that he feels so sorry for me, that I have sacrificed to take care of him. I tell him that we are both in this together. We have to care for each other because we don't have family here; it's only the two of us, so I want him to help himself because if he doesn't, I can't do anything.

We manage our life with the help of whatever we believe in. And he is getting much better. The doctor phones me after a couple of weeks. We have to go back to the hospital for Fermin's checkup of the surgery. We go and, according to the doctor, the healing process is promising, and Fermin is doing well.

I still have one week to stay home to care for him. He can eat a little better now, and he can hold food in his stomach now. As much as possible, I have to give him much softer food; vegetables, I put in the blender.

I ask him if after this week, I should take another week off. He says that he will be okay to stay home by himself, but I say that we'll see how he is doing then. He has lost lots of weight, and I know it's difficult for him to recover because he can't eat too much at a time. He doesn't want me to answer the phone when it rings because he doesn't want me to tell what happened to him if his friends phone.

One morning, about 9:00, somebody knocks on our door. When I open it, there's a couple of policemen standing there, and I say, "Yes. Can I help you?" One police officer asks me if this is where Fermin Rodriguez lives. And I say yes. He explains that one of Fermin's friends asked them to check on Fermin because he hasn't seen him for some time now. And Fermin never answers the phone.

So, I tell them that Fermin was in the hospital for surgery, and I ask them if they would like to come in. And they say not to worry , that they believe me, and they go. That is a true friend who is concerned for the well-being of another. It is Charlie who took the time and called the police to check into what happened to Fermin. Fermin is the kind of person who is so secretive. He doesn't want even his closest friend to know about his personal life and what happens.

I don't tell my family in the Philippines or Fermin's family in Spain what's going on in our life in Vancouver. I don't want them to worry about us; I know we will survive. Tomorrow is the last day that I stay home with him; I'll be off to work. He is getting much much better and is walking around the house.

I prepare food for him for tomorrow, so he can just put on the oven to heat it up, and I ask him if he can manage on his own at home when I'm at work tomorrow. He tells me not to worry too much. One week from now, we have to go to the hospital for his checkup.

I'm back to work and most of the girls ask me what happened to Fermin and I say that he's okay now. And Theresa our office coordinator says quickly that I never tell them. Fermin's surgery was very serious. I phone the hospital and tell them I am his niece, and the nurses tell me about his sickness. I'm standing there in front of everyone, and knowing all this. I am really upset because I was in the hospital every day with him, and no nurses told me this story. I say to her, how dare you snoop around the life of someone who has nothing to do with you? And the next week, she herself was in the hospital for surgery. I'm not surprised because that's the law of life: what you put out there will surely come back to you.

I can breathe a little now. When I come home, Fermin has managed to move himself around and feed himself. I just clean his body and wash his hair with a damp cloth and change his clothes. I manage our life while Fermin is in the recovery stage. Somehow my project in the Philippines must go on. I receive pictures from my brother; the outside of the house is almost done. So far, not one of the workers has quit, so there are still ten people are working; that's why it's getting done so fast.

I have my budget for building that house, so I don't worry about the expenses in sending money to finish that project. I don't feel tired after all those long weeks that I did not work. I didn't lose my strength for doing my routine at work. It's a little bit easier for me now to feel at ease. Fermin is much better now, and I am checking how our investments in the stock market are doing. At this time, more and more people are making money on the stock market, and lots of them are buying houses and condos. You can see people driving classy and fancy cars around the city.

One afternoon when I come home from work, I am surprised to meet Fermin on the elevator. I'm so glad that he can manage to go out on his own now. He tells me that he went around the block for a walk to get some fresh air, and I thank him for doing that.

As usual, I prepare everything that he needs every day before I go to work, and it is much easier for him to find it in the fridge. Next week, we have to go for his once-a-week checkup, and we are still hoping for the best result. Our life must go on in spite of this setback; the dark must come in order for us to see the light.

To keep my story short, Fermin recovers from his surgery and from that sickness. He is doing fine, although his stomach is smaller. I don't give him too much food at each meal, and he is back to normal now.

The year is 2000; I finish paying for our place, and my last expenses for my brother's house are his furniture, beds and their bedding materials, the fridge, and a two-burner stove. The house is almost finished. Only five people are left; they are just painting the inner and the outer walls of the house.

My generosity to my family has traveled far and wide the people's mouths in our community. People talk about me, saying that they have never heard of anyone giving that kind of help and making such sacrifices for their sisters and brother, and they can hardly believe it. But, for me, a promise is a promise to keep, not to break. That's the reason why, from now on, I don't open my mouth to say things that I know I can't do it—because my words are my honor; it's as simple as that.

I put seven children through college and university. Some have done well and others have not, but somehow, they manage their lives, to live on their own with their own skills to survive, and I'm out of it now.

As for me and Fermin, as the saying goes, "If you take care of me, I'll take care of you." Fermin was able to buy his dream car, a Porsche Baxter. I have to include this in my writing, not to brag, but to explain that what anyone desires and dreams, he or she can have it when the time is right —because our desire creates action; after that, it's the materialization of what you really want. That's what happened in Fermin's case.

As you can see, my younger brother and sisters in spiritual awakening, life is easy if we can just look deeper inside ourself. We already have all the tools to make our lives easier at our disposal , but we always look in a different direction. That's the reason why we are trapped in failure of our own doing. But that's what life is. Each one of us must find our leadings, but now is the time to minimize the hunger and homelessness of this world of ours. Why is it that so many of us are so poor? And only a few are so wealthy?

It's because the wrong belief of so many of us poor people that if you are rich you are doing something wrong. You are not honest in your dealings, which allows you to accumulate your wealth, and you are not a religious person or wanting to be one, and this is wrong. We are all divine spirits experiencing the human body. We are all negative thinkers, and it's time for us to claim it.

Please awaken to your royal heritage for we are all one. I am in you, and you are in me. We must not think separately for the I am and me, is also in you and in me, which is our "consciousness" and our reality. The first truth for each one of us is when we are born, and the only truth for each one of us is when we finish our work in this lifetime. We all come from spirit, we are spirit, and we go back to spirit.

Fermin and I have survived our trials. He is enjoying his life, getting attached to his baby car; during my days off, we drive long distances in the USA and in Okanagan. Life is much easier now that almost of my projects are done. The support that I send to my siblings now is only for food and the expenses for their children to go to college.

We don't travel much outside the country because Fermin said hates to travel abroad. He always says that he lost a number of years off his life from the food, the loss of sleep, traveling around, and catching flights. It makes him sick, and that's the reason why we seldom travel. But I always go to the Philippines once a year for a month.

After seven years of having his Porsche Baxter S, he let it go, and I cry because I am attached to it too. For sure, I'll miss it, but he says he is going to buy a new model, the Porsche Cayman S. He does in the year 2008, and I love it too. Fermin has good taste in material things, even in paintings. He is very particular about the color and design of his clothes and shoes.

As for me, I still love my job and have resumed my overtime routine. It seems like I'm more energetic now that I am getting older. My appetite for my work never slows down. I think the secret in life is to surround yourself with beautiful things, especially flowers and paintings, in your living place to give you inspiration and to boost your good health.

FINDING "ME"

By the year 2010, I ask Fermin to travel by himself to visit his family and relatives in the North of Spain, and I'm glad he didoes. He stays there for couple of months, and I don't mind at all because it's difficult for me to persuade him to travel. As for me, being alone for two months in the comfort of life allows me to concentrate my focus on my work and my thoughts on saving more for our retirement. I don't want to repeat what I did when I was still at home with my parents. I worked in the factory for more than five years and gave all my salary to my mother for their expenses. By the time, I needed money, no one could give it to me. That's the big mistake that I made, so I learned not to do it again.

I have stayed here in my work for a very long time now. It's not that it's difficult for me to find other work, but because I love what I do and my salary here is much much higher than anywhere else, so why bother looking elsewhere. I don't know if I can retire here, but who knows? That's way far ahead. So, life continues here; I work and love every minute of it.

Fermin arrives after a two-month break, and he looks so alert and happy. I know how it feels to be in different environment and surroundings; it makes you feel alive again. He brings me lots of goodies and he loves to bring presents to his friends too. Two of his nieces have sent beautiful letters to me, but I can understand only a little because the writing is in Spanish. They ask me when they will be able to see me and how much longer it will be. I know they are good people, but my plan is to see them when I retire.

There are lots of changes at my work place; some of the management have retired, and the place had been sold to a new owner. In our department, there are no changes because most of my coworkers have been here even longer than me. Some of them were hired during the opening of this place, so our work is steady. We have good days and bad days, but we get along.

In 2013, the passing of my friend Greta is really a big blow to me. Although she was not working here with us anymore, we still communicated with each other and her life was the ideal life. I looked up to her life and I applied it to mine. She, with her friend Candy, had a beautiful town home close to Metrotown. According to Greta, she and Candy had been close friends and neighbor when they were growing up. She was in and out of the hospital, and she was only fifty-nine years old.

All my coworkers ask me what happened to her, but I just tell them that she was secretive and didn't want me to tell anyone; that they understand. I'm trying to shake off from my thoughts her life story but what a sad one that what's the point, We struggle so hard to have a better life, but out of the blue, we are all left behind It's hard and unfair of life, but that's the reality, and we have to accept it.

Fermin and I continue with our routine. He has been retired for quite some time now, so I tell him not to worry about anything. Enjoy every day of your life. We have to do what we want to do because life has no guarantee. It can be taken from us any time of day or night. I'm still working, but I slow down with my overtime.

In the mornings when I am working, I always prepare our breakfast. Then, when I go walking, Fermin has to go with me for his morning walk around Stanley Park; that's his morning walking routine, and it makes him healthier and fitter. And for me, that's most of my commute to work because we are only fifteen to twenty minutes away. How fortunate we are that we can live in the downtown area.

FINDING "ME"

In February of 2014, I go back home to see how my project looks. How happy and satisfied I am with the finished work of my brother house and the paint outside the house. I like it very much, and the furniture they picked really matches with the space of the living room. Well, it seems like they won a jackpot lottery ticket with this beautiful house. How lucky my siblings were because of Fermin's and my generosity and because of my promise to my mother such a very long time ago. I had to keep it because my words are me.

I feel a little sad because Fermin was not able to see all our projects here because he doesn't want to travel here, and I can't force him to come with me right now. He is a part of what I've done because if he hadn't allow me to spent our money, how could I afford all these expenses? There is no way I could have done this by myself. But here it is: all done, and I am free. Sometimes life is beautiful and sometimes not, but it is, what it is.

You can see, my younger brothers and sisters in spiritual awakening, that what happens when someone is sad doesn't mean that we will react the same and lose the hope of living, of striving to improve our own situation in life. We must continue living and, most of all, enjoying the journey. Don't be concerned about your destination. Most of us don't even recognize our Higher Self who guides us all along, teaching us where and what to do for our own good. We think that we are always in control of everything, but we are doing without knowing that the I am and me in each one of us are the only ones in charge. Every good thing that happens to each one of us, not only that but the actual doer, thinker giver and taker in each one of us, for he is the impersonal life that we never recognize and realize that we are all one and not separate from us. I am in you, you are in me. The truth is that we are but one. When our own consciousness and the universal consciousness are connected, we become one—the term born again is sometimes used. Until that thing happens, it's very hard for us to accept it as true, but it will happen. The time goes by. Each one of us connects; it happens to each one of us individually.

In my own calculation, we have saved enough. With my income and Fermin retirement pension, we can live comfortably on what we have. I mention to Fermin that I feel inside of me that it's about time for me to retire. I'm still working everyday and don't slow down at all. I still do overtime when they ask me to.

Six months later, I find myself at the door of my manager's office, telling him that I am retiring, and he asks me why. He says that I am still young, and I say that there's no reason. I just feel it's time for me to retire.

I don't know exactly what triggers me to decide to retire—the passing of my friend Greta or the emptiness inside me that I feel. What is the point of all these material things that we acquire and accumulate. Is this all there is? Why I don't feel happy now? I feel that something I want to have is missing, and it seems so close to me and yet it's so far away, but I don't know what it is.

On August 8, 2014, the company that I have worked with for twenty-seven years gives me a retirement party. Fifty-eight people attend the gathering. My coworkers give me lots of gifts and money, and our general manager gives me an iPad. I don't know anything about electronic things, but I have to learn now that I'm not working anymore. According to one of the girls, they spent more than $500 for the restaurant alone. But I surprise each one of them. I give each one an envelope with some money, so I

FINDING "ME"

spend almost the same amount as they did. They ask why I have to do this? But I say only that life is give and take, that's why. So, that was that, the end of my working days. I worked in one place for twenty-seven years.

Fermin and I, we book tickets for Spain. At last, I am able to meet his family. They are good, beautiful people. They accept me as one of their family, and we have a good time. We travel to so many places, and I'm so amazed by the mountains upon mountains that are so beautiful. I have never seen anything like this scenery any other place that I traveled to before. It's so different here. We stay for a month, and for sure, I'll go back there.

I have a different schedule now. I don't have to get up so early; all my time is mine now. Every morning after breakfast, Fermin and I go for a long walk around Stanley Park. It takes us one and a half hours at just a normal walk. We go driving around the city for sightseeing and come home at night. We don't do much, but I don't feel bored being at home now. I have much time for cleaning that I missed when I was working, so I can do that and more now. I still go to the Philippines every year for a month, and Fermin just stays home because he hates to travel far away.

We enjoy each other's company now that both of us are no longer working. We have a few friends in the building where we live, and there are times when we get together to go to a restaurant for dinner.

Our neighbor John owns the travel agency where we got our tickets for Spain. We meet him every morning in the lobby when we go for our walk. He goes running at the same time as we go walking, so we just say good morning and go on our way. But, for some reason, we haven't seen him for quite some time now. Fermin and I we don't pay attention to that because we think maybe we are just missing him in the morning.

But one morning when we go down, he is there at the counter, talking to the security guard and he says to us, "Don't you guys come to my shop anymore? I was in the hospital for six months." He continues, "one day, I am walking down the street on my way to work, and a few steps away from my shop, I step on banana peel, and I'm flat on the ground. I just got back to work one month ago, but I moved. I'm here now, close to home, My shop is in Roger's building across from this building on the second floor.

One week later, the security tells us that one afternoon about 2:00, John came home. He looked so yellow and couldn't open the entrance door. He went up to his suite and, according to the security guard, the next morning, he's gone. Fermin and I are so saddened by this news. It's just as quick as the blink of an eye. We send our prayers for a quick journey for his soul and peace.

So much goes on in this building nowadays. Just a few weeks ago, I heard someone telling a story inside the elevator that, they saw one person sleeping with a blanket in the hallway of the seventh floor. He told the security guard in the lobby, but when security checked, it was a dead man. I have never heard such a story in my life, especially happening in this building. We have lived here for more than twenty years now, and this is happening now? I'm a little uneasy living here now.

I tell Fermin about the story of this guy in the hallway, and he was surprised that no one in security is telling anyone. They are so secretive because of the reputation of the building; otherwise, no one will live here anymore.

FINDING "ME"

One morning on our way to Stanley Park for our routine walk is one of the homeless guys. He is running after me and asks me to buy food for him; so Fermin and I stop and tell him that we don't have money because we are just walking. He says that he has money, so I ask him why he doesn't go there and buy his food. He says that they don't allow him in the store because he is so dirty and smelly. So, I ask Fermin to stay on the side of the road to wait for me. I get the guy's money and run about one block away to a 7-Eleven store and buy him a small cup of coffee, two bran muffins, and two donuts— and he still has one dollar left.

There are mornings that I prepare some fruit and two pieces of bread with a small bottle of water, and I carry them with me during our morning walk. Luckily enough, he is still in the same spot, and I give the food to him. He tells me not to do this because he has to move sometimes; otherwise, the police will take his cart away. So, I stop doing this. This buying food for him happens at least three times more. This homeless guy is a Chinese person, and I can feel something in my guts that seems like I'm being tested for my reaction to these people.

One thing leads to another. One day, I meet Mr. Eddie Yeo, our neighbour and friend. He is from Singapore and lives alone in Vancouver as a permanent resident. He asks me to help him pay his bill on the computer because he must apply for the renewal of his PR every five years. I tell him that I can do that, but I can't get a receipt because I don't have a printer. I ask my other neighbor if she can help me to help him, and we do, and he is very happy for this.

That's what life is all about. If we can do something that will help someone, we must do it because someday we might need help. We are all human beings and that's what we are here for. My Chinese neighbor, I always help her by looking after her mail when she goes to China for six months, and I ask her to help me when it comes to doing things on the computer because she is good for that. That's life—give and take.

It's still October, but I'm already looking for a plane ticket for the Philippines. I am planning a home visit by April, and I got a ticket that's really a very good bargain. This year, the cost is much lower than I usually pay. Being retired gives me freedom to stay there for at least a month. I don't want to stay longer than that, especially because Fermin is not with me.

Life is so beautiful and easy if you plan and work according to your choices. For the life style we want to live, we have a kind of direction, like a map, that we have to follow. I know that every one of us has that kind of instinct inside of us. That's the beauty; you know that you can't be wrong, that you are on the right path.

December is here already, so there are holidays to plan for, but we don't do so much of that now, especially since I am not working anymore. I don't have to make any preparation anymore. So, I guess, it's just me and Fermin this time. Our neighbour is in China right now and will not be back until June.

I call our friend Mr. Yeo, but no one answers, so I think he must traveling abroad. We have a quiet Christmas this year, but I'm looking forward to my travel in April, and I'm excited. In January, Mr. Yeo calls us and he tells me that he had the flu for the whole month of December. I say, "I called you to say Happy New Year, but you didn't answer, so we thought you were away."

I ask him if he had seen the doctor, and he says no, because his doctor passed away four years ago. I say that there must be some doctors that have taken over his patients and ask if he would like me to help him find one. I tell Fermin that we have to help him and he says yes. So, I go and look for a walk-in clinic close to our area, and I found one. I go up to his place and knock on his door, and he opens the door. He doesn't look that bad, not very ill.

I tell him about the clinic, and I ask if he would like me to take him there. He says that he can manage to go there by himself. I say that he must be sure to see the doctor, and he says yes. So, I go down home, and I tell Fermin that Mr. Yeo wants to see the doctor by himself.

Later on that day, he gives us a call again, telling us that he has a follow-up checkup tomorrow. I ask him if he has something to eat for supper, and he says he doesn't feel like eating. I say that I'll make him some nice soup. He says no because he has some in the fridge.

I ask him if it's alright for Fermin and I come for a visit after we eat our dinner, and he says yes. We go up after our dinner and we talk. He looks like he's getting better, and I ask how he feels. He says his whole body is aching, especially his right shoulder. I ask if he is smoking and he says very lightly. I say there is no such thing as lightly when it comes to smoking. It is still smoking, and I say that I hope he can stop it, and he is just silent.

I suggest to him that we can phone one of his nieces to come and visit him. He says no because they have their own lives, and they are working. It's difficult for them to come here. I ask him if he has a will, and he says, "I don't need that. I am not dying yet. I will get better soon,"

I say, "I know, but you know what? You should make one sooner than later because everyone dies. We hope for the best, but we also should prepare for the worst. Okay? Because it will help you, and it will help your family later. I don't wish for bad things to happen, but we just do our work. I'll help you find a lawyer." And he agrees.

To make the story short, I wasn't able to travel home. I phone my sister to tell her that my plan is canceled because of some circumstances that I can't ignore, and she understands me. Fermin and I bring him to the hospital, and on April 15, 2017, at 12:03 in the afternoon, he passes away. I do everything as best I can for him and for his family. I am not sure what is happening to me, but I don't question. I remember the words in the Bible, "you did not choose me, but I have chosen you".

You can see, my younger brother's and sister's in spiritual awakening, you don't have to be scared; you don't have to worry; you don't have to be anxious for anything. Just be joyful every day and be happy. Don't get mad for whatever station of life you are in right now, just breathe one breath at a time. With the limitless flow of life that our universe is supplying us with every moment of our life, just keep that desire and dreams alive inside. Water it with laughter and happy feelings with every breath you take and, without your knowing, it will bloom like a rose. Everything will change, and you will have the courage to make good choices, take action, have gratitude, and practice honesty with yourself. Nothing can go wrong; you are guided in the right path.

Fermin and I have lived here in the downtown area for twenty-two years now, and both of us feel the urge to move out of this place. It seems to me that the service of this place to us is already done. It happens quickly. I dig out all our stuff; that which we don't want to carry with us, I box it up and send to the Philippines. I find a place to move and clean up everything.

I give thanks and prayers for the service of this place, and pass on the good fortune of this home to someone who will live here. It will continue on and on. But, of course, most of good luck and good fortune we carry with us, and the most is inside each of us.

Our life completely changed, not in a bad way, but different. We enjoyed each other's company, but at the same time, gave freedom and space for both of us. That made us stick around for a very long time now.

One morning, after our breakfast, we are both sitting down in our living room when, suddenly, I smell a beautiful sweet smell of perfume. It's so strong, and I ask Fermin if he smells the sweet smell, and he says no. I am so surprised, why only me? I remember right away the date of Mr. Eddie Yeo's birthday, and it's August 21, 1939. I ask Fermin if he can bring flowers when he comes home later that day and he does.

The place and area where we are living is completely different than where we used to be. We are not far from Downtown, only fifteen minutes away by bus. The stillness and quietness of the surrounding trees, many that have been here for more than one hundred years. It is so amazing—like I'm walking in the forest; it's so beautiful.

We still do our early morning, one-hour walks. We seldom meet people on the street. I guess people in this area are not early risers, trees upon trees on both sides of the road is completely different scenery.

One night, I am thinking that, since I am still capable of doing something, I can still make some extra income and can continue sending help to my family way back home in the Philippines. I fall into a deep sleep, and I hear this little sweet voice saying, "What are you worrying about? You are not in charge of them. I am. Me. And I am in charge of you. Will you help me, so they can feel me inside of their being?"

I am awake; it is 2:00 a.m., and I say to myself, "This is the truth that I have been looking for, for a very long time. When I was young, this was one of my desires—that I would find the truth myself one day. Wow! Why now?" I have no doubt that from now on, I will have no questions because I trust myself.

If I've been given this knowledge of truth, I too should give, for even though I don't go to the church or temple, I know the words from the old book of teaching, "Those who have received must give."

All the selflessness that I have demonstrated since I have grown up, little did I know that it's my passport in finding the kingdom of God and Heaven or Light and Love. Whatever we call it, we can't find it anywhere but inside our being, through our hearts. For heaven is not a place outside of us, but inside the inner core of our hearts.

It is when I completely focus on others that I abandon the needs of myself. In that long journey, I found me, the I am in me. And that is why, my younger brothers and sisters in spiritual awakening, each one of us has our own way, our own path to follow until we find our Real Self, the Truth of us, our inner self, The Higher Intelligence, which is the real you. The truth is, we are all one in everyone and everything that is.

FINDING "ME"

If I had known then what I know now, I wouldn't have had to travel the long highways and byways or toil with tears and sweat on my brow, climbing the mountains of my life. So, my younger brothers and sisters, I hope I've given you a map of ideas; I share them with all of you who are ready to learn that inside, not outside, of you is where the magic of life is, where the endless happiness is, in the light and love, so you too can shine brightly.

I hope that you have enjoyed reading my story.

I dedicate this book to me, that after decade upon decade of treading and swimming the dark and muddy water of adversity, I am able to emerge into the light of the bright star that shines over me.

INOCENCIA TUPAS MALUNES

May 21, 2020

Dear Sophie & Dan.

Good things comes from small package. I hope this one will prove it. Enjoy.

[signature]